In God
We Doubt

In a broadcasting career spanning forty-five years JOHN HUMPHRYS has reported from all over the world for the BBC and presented its frontline news programmes on both radio and television. He was a foreign correspondent and the first journalist to present the *Nine O'Clock News*. John has won a string of national awards and been described as a 'national treasure' – all of which he attributes to longevity and luck. He presents Radio 4's *Today* programme and BBC2's *Mastermind*.

Also by John Humphrys

Beyond Words

Lost for Words

The Great Food Gamble

Devil's Advocate

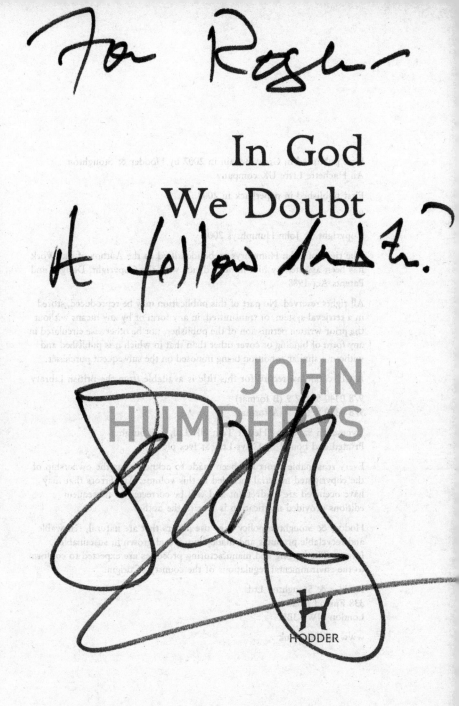

In God
We Doubt

JOHN
HUMPHRYS

HODDER

First published in Great Britain in 2007 by Hodder & Stoughton
An Hachette Livre UK company

First published in paperback in 2008

9

A CIP catalogue record for this title is available from the British Library

978 0340 95127 9 (B format)
978 0340 97673 9 (A format)

Typeset in Sabon by Hewer Text UK Ltd, Edinburgh
Printed and bound by Clays Ltd, St Ives plc

Every reasonable effort has been made to acknowledge the ownership of
the copyrighted material included in this volume. Any errors that may
have occurred are inadvertent and will be corrected in subsequent
editions provided notification is sent to the author.

Hodder & Stoughton policy is to use papers that are natural, renewable
and recyclable products and made from wood grown in sustainable
forests. The logging and manufacturing processes are expected to conform
to the environmental regulations of the country of origin.

Hodder & Stoughton Ltd
338 Euston Road
London NW1 3BH

www.hodder.co.uk

Dedication

I started giving serious thought to religion a couple of years ago when I was in the process of setting up a trust fund to raise money for small charities in poor countries that help people at the very bottom of the ladder – usually children with no parents and no hope.

The people who run them have enormous enthusiasm and energy. What they don't have is much money or the ability to raise it: no swanky offices staffed with marketing and fundraising teams. Hence the Kitchen Table Charities Trust (www.kitchentablecharities.org). We raise money and make grants to these tiny charities around the world so that they can do their amazing work. The KTCT has no paid staff, but we've managed to help nearly a hundred small charities and want to do much more.

Raising money is never easy, but it's nothing compared with what these people do. Many of them dedicate their lives to caring for orphaned children; setting up little hospitals to remove cataracts or cure club feet; organising loan schemes so widowed mothers can run tiny businesses; giving street children an education or training them in skills like carpentry.

These people are changing lives and they're doing it out of love. Some believe in God; some don't. They're good people and that's why this book is dedicated to them.

Acknowledgements

I could fill pages thanking all those who have helped me write this book simply by writing to me and talking to me about their faith – or lack of it. Apart from the help their letters have given me it has been an immensely rewarding and enriching experience. I'm grateful to them all.

But I must single out a few people. Giles Fraser is in the best tradition of troublesome priests and I enjoyed our arguments over the kitchen table. I'm grateful to many old friends including Rod Liddle, John Wakefield, Patrick Holden and Peter Seggar for their (mostly) moral support and encouragement. Fiona Hamilton helped with both research and reassurance.

My biggest thanks to two of my children: my daughter Catherine and my son Owen. Catherine brought order out of the chaos of my letter mountains. If any newspaper is looking for a Letters Page editor, she's proved her worth. And Owen, at the age of six, showed me that you don't need a degree in divinity to express some pretty clear views on God.

Contents

Contents

The Challenge

In the green hills of west Wales, home to more sheep than people, there is a small museum that attracts very few visitors but deserves a mention in any self-respecting book about God. It is dedicated to the history of wool.

One of the things you will learn there is that for many years human urine was an important part of the process of preparing the raw wool for the spinners. Locals were paid a penny a gallon to deliver their waste to their local factory. Unless, that is, they were Methodists – in which case they were paid twopence a gallon. This was because Methodists did not (in those days, anyway) drink alcohol. So their urine was of a purer form and thus more valuable to the processors. The message is obvious: faith in God pays; it delivers clear benefits. Or it did for a brief period in our history. And now?

Well, that rather depends on whom you believe and what you believe – which is the point of this book. I would hate any potential reader to think I am about to answer the greatest unanswered question of all time. Or even try to.

Atheists of the Richard Dawkins stripe know that God does not exist. To believe that he does is a dangerous delusion.

Believers know with equal certainty that not only does he exist but if you embrace him your life will be transformed, you will overcome suffering and death and you will go to heaven – an even better return on your investment than an extra penny for a gallon of pee.

As for me: I don't know. This book is aimed at the millions of people like me who have given God a lot of thought over the years and have managed to come to no definite conclusion but would very much like to. They probably seem slightly ashamed of their doubt. After all, it's the easy option, isn't it? Well, no, it isn't. It's quite the opposite.

I'll tell you what's easy. Atheism for a start. Anyone with the enquiring mind of a bright child can see that the case made for God by the three great monotheistic religions – Judaism, Christianity and Islam – is riddled with holes. Christopher Hitchens rumbled God when he was nine – or so he tells us in his book on atheism, *God Is Not Great*. His teacher, Mrs Watts, had demonstrated to the class how powerful and generous God was by pointing out that he had made the trees and the grass green – exactly the colour that is most restful to our eyes – instead of something ghastly like purple. Young Hitchens was appalled:

> My little ankle-straps curled with embarrassment for her . . . I simply knew that my teacher had managed to get everything wrong in just two sentences. The eyes were adjusted to nature, and not the other way about.

It's as simple as that, you see. One 'pious old trout of a teacher' (his unkind description) managed to turn one little boy into a fierce scourge of religion without even knowing it. How Hitchens would have turned out if he'd had a different teacher with an approach more suited to such a little clever-clogs we shall never know. Probably the same. You don't have to be very clever to spot the flaws in the God argument.

It's easy being a fundamentalist, too. Mostly you don't have to think at all. Once you have bought the whole package everything fits. If you believe every word in the Bible or acknowledge that the Koran is literally the word of God, well, that's it. Everything follows from that. You might be a little puzzled at how God managed to create the world in six days and take a day off on Sunday to cut the grass, but if it says he did in the Bible, it must be true. Or you might be a little less gullible where the details are concerned but still accept the core message. Or God might have appeared to you personally and settled the argument. Either way, religious fundamentalism is a pretty comfortable perch to occupy once you've settled there.

Doubt is altogether different. There are two questions for agnostics. The one that gets to the heart of it was not, I'm sorry to say, asked by me on the *Today* programme or by any of my colleagues. It was asked about three hundred years ago by the German philosopher and mathematician Gottfried Leibniz and has never been improved upon. It is this:

Why is there something rather than nothing?

Believers have no problem in answering it: it's because God decided there should be. Believers who also happen to be brilliant scientists – like the theoretical physicist John Polkinghorne – say the

same but take longer to say it. Atheists don't know
– however clever they may be. What they do know
is that it can't have been God because there's no
such being. Most are pretty confident that, since
humans are becoming ever more knowledgeable,
we shall find the answer one day. Incidentally,
that's almost a religious belief, isn't it?

The question that follows from Leibniz for
doubters is:

If it *was* because of God, what sort of God?

For the purpose of this book I am concerned with
the monotheistic religions. Their God seems to be
exactly the sort of person you'd want your daughter to marry if he were human: kind, merciful,
immensely loving; all-powerful and just. But if you
are a doubter you look at the world around you
and say something along the lines of 'You're telling
me God is like that and yet *this* is what he created?
You must be joking!'

It has always seemed to me that the default
position for the human condition is that there is
'something out there'. Dunno what, we shrug, but
this can't all be one big accident, can it? It is
usually said in an almost wistful way, more an
expression of hope than of belief. We want to feel
there's a purpose to our lives, that we've been put

5

on earth as part of some divine plan, and if not divine then at least pre-ordained for some reason beyond our understanding. We want to believe that there's more to life than this brief passage and, with a bit of luck, that there might even be something nice waiting for us when we finally turn up our toes.

Otherwise what's the point? We struggle along as best we can for seven or eight decades – a bit more if we're lucky – then fade out of the picture. Maybe we'll do a bit of good somewhere along the way and leave the world a tiny bit better than we found it. Maybe we won't. Maybe we'll be mourned, and maybe those we leave behind will offer up a silent prayer of thanks that the old bugger's gone at last. Not very comforting, is it? And that's partly the point. We want desperately to be comforted – and we fear being alone.

Biology may dictate that we are all unique individuals and some of us may have egos as big as the Milky Way, but we all want to believe we're part of something bigger than ourselves. Science-fiction writers know how to tap into this – perhaps the deepest of all our fears. I'm not thinking of that weird alien that jumps out of Sigourney Weaver's chest and goes scuttling off into some dark corner of the spaceship. That's scary, but it's also very silly. No, the real nightmare is being cast adrift in space. The line connecting you to the mother ship suddenly snaps and you drift away into the infinite emptiness, knowing that no one can come and get you. Ever.

The alternative to the 'something out there' scenario is that we simply evolved from the primordial sludge and will eventually be submerged back into it – or vanish from the earth in a more spectacular way when the sun implodes. It is less comforting but a lot more plausible. Belief in intelligent design is based on faith and hope, with a large dollop of wishful thinking thrown in. Acceptance of evolution is based on reason and science. We know so much more than we have ever known about what makes us the curious creatures we are.

As Matt Ridley tells us in his book *Genome*, there are a hundred trillion cells in the human body. Each cell has a nucleus and each nucleus has two sets of the human genome. Each genome contains enough information to fill a library of about five thousand books. If all the chromosomes in a single body were laid out end to end they would stretch a hundred billion miles. Our brains alone have a billion nerve cells.

It's not easy to get a grip on this. If you're a doubter you can't help wondering why God didn't just cut to the chase when he set about creating us. Why bother with the rather dull primordial-sludge stage and all those years when we either swam or crawled or crept around the place without being able to offer so much as a cheery 'Good morning!' to one another? Why didn't he just set up some great assembly line and churn us out, possibly equipped with built-in television screens between brains and eyes and iPods instead of ears? It's perfectly clear that we shall eventually stop communicating with each other in any meaningful sense anyway, so it would have been far more sensible to make it possible for humans to live in their own hermetically sealed worlds right from the beginning. And if God decided we should all be distinct individuals, surely he could have programmed the divine computer accordingly?

These may be difficult questions for agnostics – but not for believers. God is infallible. Supernatural. The supreme intelligence who put it all together. He is not obedient to the laws of nature for the simple reason that he designed them. He is the creator who made everything and everyone and is still out there keeping an eye on it. Whatever happens is happening because ultimately God willed it and it must be right – because he is God. He will punish us when we sin and he might reward us when we are good. Either way, he listens to our prayers and may intervene on our behalf at some stage – possibly in this life or perhaps in the next.

All of this is accepted by mainstream believers in the monotheistic faiths. To challenge the basics would be to challenge the omnipotence and even the existence of God. He is almighty or he is nothing.

For fully-paid-up, card-carrying fundamentalists, it is simpler still. Not even the tricky theological questions apply. After hours of arguing with an evangelical philosopher about the existence of God, I asked him how he would have coped if I had managed to prove that his arguments were false. Would it have destroyed or even dented his faith in God? No, he said, it would not. He had occasional doubts, but he believed in God, always would and that was that. He patiently pointed out to me, as so many did while I was researching this book, that faith meant exactly what it says. If it could be proved it would not be faith.

Hardline fundamentalists display an almost pitying approach to doubters that seems calculated to drive us round the bend. It causes more moderate believers to tear their hair out, too.

But what is a 'moderate' believer? They will insist, for instance, that no one believes any longer that we should obey the Bible's injunction to kill a child who swears at his parent, and they recoil from some of the more savage punishments for the unfaithful ordered up by God in the Old Testament. Christians will refer you to the New Testament and 'gentle Jesus'. But Jesus himself accepted the laws of the Old Testament and warned that anyone who did not could never enter the kingdom of heaven. That's what it says in the New Testament and that's what, if we accept the word of its Gospels, we must believe.

This book is based partly on my own personal experience and, inevitably, on my own prejudices. I have been both believer and non-believer in my time. Because of the terrible things I have seen as a reporter over the years – wars, famines, disasters – I suspect I have spent most of my spiritual journey looking for reasons to satisfy myself that God does not exist. To buttress my scepticism. Those reasons are not hard to find. Maybe 'excuses' is a better word.

My Radio 4 series *Humphrys in Search of God*, broadcast in the autumn of 2006, had a bigger impact on me than I had expected. It was not that my interviewees – leaders in their own religions – proved the case for God to my intellectual satisfaction. They did not. In fact, they raised at least as many questions as they answered. That is hardly surprising. It's not easy to compress nearly four thousand years of theology into three half-hour interviews – not even when you work for a programme that routinely asks its guests to summarise the causes and outcomes of both world wars 'very briefly if you will, please, because we're just about out of time'. Well, there's plenty of time for this debate.

Monotheistic religion has survived a few millennia and, assuming our species lasts that long, will probably survive another few in some shape or form. But it would be foolish to underestimate the ferocity of the campaign being waged by its enemies. As Dawkins writes in *The God Delusion*:

> If this book works as I intend, religious readers who open it will be atheists when they put it down.

Books such as his have been pouring off the printing presses like Spitfires leaving the assembly lines in 1939, written by some of the world's leading thinkers: Daniel Dennett, Lewis Wolpert, A. C. Grayling, Sam Smith, Christopher Hitchens,

Michel Onfray. They are the masters of many disciplines – you could paper the walls of an aircraft hangar with their degrees and qualifications – admired and envied throughout academia and journalism for their knowledge and intellect. They argue their case, as you would expect, with skill, wit and passion. But ultimately they fail – at least for me.

Reading them all is a bit like gorging on your favourite chocolate, which, in my case, happens to be black with a punishingly high cocoa content and some nuts to give it crunch. The first nibble is immensely satisfying – it leaves a wonderfully bitter aftertaste – but the second isn't as good as the first and the third isn't . . . Well, you get the drift. You know what the next bite will taste like – just like the first one but a bit less so.

The tone of the atheist diatribes might differ – Wolpert is altogether more polite and moderate than, say, Hitchens – but not the content. Actually, Hitchens makes the Taliban look tame. His book *God Is Not Great* is sub-titled *Religion Poisons Everything*. Not just lots of things or even most things or even almost everything. It's everything. Mr Hitchens is not a man to do things by half. Religion, he says, is:

Violent, irrational, intolerant, allied to racism and tribalism and bigotry, invested in ignorance and hostile to free inquiry, contemptuous of women and coercive towards children.

It probably gives you dandruff and bad breath too.

Hyperbole aside, it's hard not to be impressed by the atheists' argument. Logic and science are on their side. No less a figure than Frederick the Great of Prussia is said to have described Christianity as 'an old metaphysical fiction, stuffed with fables, contradictions and absurdities'.

When it comes to ammunition, as I have already suggested, modern atheists have more than enough. The Devil not only has the best tunes, but the best arguments.

Jewish scholars try to get round the most weird stuff in the Old Testament by printing interpretations of what the writers might have meant, translated into a modern context. There is often a lot more interpretation than original text.

Christian theologians make great demands on our credulity too. Their attempts to explain away the yawning chasms between the messages delivered to the faithful about the nature of God and the reality of their everyday lives often verge on the embarrassing. They mostly rest on the notion of free will. But if the God of the Bible truly is a God of mercy then, as militant atheists delight in pointing out, satire has indeed had its day.

The rational atheist has science at his disposal, and the thing about good science is that it can be proved. The devout have the scriptures and they cannot prove their case. This presents the defenders of religion with a sizeable problem. For Jews there can be no question that God chose Abraham as his instrument to get the whole thing going. For Christian apologists it is essential that Jesus rose again. For Muslims it is a given that God spoke directly to Muhammad. You either believe these claims or you do not.

If a sceptic demands proof, then in the end the faithful have little choice but to hide behind the door marked 'mystery'. We are told that since God is so much greater than the puny mortals he created, we cannot presume to understand all his works. It's like the old Superman comics: with one bound, he was free! Convincing? Hardly.

So, religion appears to be a vulnerable target waiting to be demolished by a few well-aimed tank shells. What the atheist militia have actually unleashed in the past couple of years has been a blitzkrieg. You almost want to intercede like a referee in a boxing match between two unequal opponents and plead with the champion: 'Enough! The job is done. Please stop now.' Almost, but not quite, because the job has not been done – not yet anyway. The much-battered opponent has not been defeated and there is a good reason for that.

In every battle the successful general chooses the ground on which he will fight. The ground chosen by the atheists is the existence of a supernatural God. No doubt some agnostics, tempted by the idea of signing up to the faith, will listen to them and conclude that the case for God is pretty indefensible. That is a victory of a sort. But there is another battlefield and another enemy. This enemy is not the existence of God; it is the existence of belief in God.

It is an inconvenient reality for the militant atheists that an awful lot of people do happen to believe. This fact of belief – and not the hypothesis of the existence of God – is what they really need to be aiming their big guns at. But it's a much more difficult target. It is one thing to line up one's sights on a demonstrably idiotic claim by a bunch of creationists who march around with a big bull's-eye attached to their backsides. It is quite another to attack the army of quiet believers. These are the people who no more think the earth was created a few thousand years ago than they think the tooth fairy still pays regular visits to their bedroom. They may even harbour grave doubts about the authenticity of the scriptures and question such fundamental Christian beliefs as the resurrection of Jesus, but they have no doubt that the God they believe in is as real in their lives as their children or their parents.

We are at an interesting point in the story of religion in Europe. For two thousand years Christianity had things pretty much all its own way, whatever the setbacks. When Martin Luther nailed his manifesto to a church door in Saxony in 1517 he challenged the might of the Roman Catholic Church. The Reformation, which produced the Protestant Church, was born and the Bible – not the Catholic priests, who were so often corrupt – was seen as the sole source of truth.

A couple of centuries later the European Enlightenment put paid to an unquestioning acceptance of religious dogma. Centuries of superstition and fairy stories masquerading as learning were exposed for the nonsense they were. In his book *The Pursuit of Glory*, Tim Blanning writes that the great philosopher David Hume went to Paris and found himself in a drawing room with eighteen other guests, all of whom were atheists. Such a thing would have been inconceivable in an earlier century. But religion was still an immensely powerful force.

Then in the nineteenth century Charles Darwin appeared on the scene. In the past few years, some important aspects of Darwinism have been questioned by serious scientists, but his theory on evolution by natural selection changed everything. The Church rallied, though, and the Victorians had a grand old time taking Jesus to the savages – whether they wanted him or not.

The twentieth century was a real test of faith and belief in a God of peace. We killed and maimed each other with an efficiency and enthusiasm unparalleled in the history of humanity. As the century closed, and with most of us failing even to realise what was going on, another monster surfaced: Islamic extremism.

The twenty-first century came of age on 11 September 2001. Nineteen Muslims, with the name of their God on their lips, murdered three thousand Americans. Extreme Islamists claim it was an act of holy war, part of the fight to restore the power of the ancient caliphate and rescue it from 'crusader' domination. In his book *The Islamist*, the Muslim writer Ed Husain draws a clear distinction between Muslims and Islamists – such as the members of Hizb ut-Tahrir – who call for a totalitarian, expansionist Islamist state that has *jihad* as foreign policy . . . 'confronting the West and killing non-Muslims and Muslims'. He told me how easy it has become for such extremists to gain a hold on the imagination of credulous young men. He should know. He was once one of them. Now he has become a target of their threats. Whatever else they may have achieved, the zealots have given militant atheists yet more ammunition. Isn't this what religion does, they say, create endless conflict in the name of God?

So the atheists are on the march armed with much logic and even more righteous indignation at the horror of religion and determined, at the very least, to weaken its grip on the national debate. Christian leaders, they point out, have enjoyed a remarkably privileged existence in this increasingly secular nation. We have automatically turned to the priests and the bishops for our moral guidance and sought their views on the great ethical issues. Twenty-six bishops of the Anglican Church are still guaranteed seats in Parliament, even though the House of Lords has been reformed in other respects. Religious schools, which teach the Bible

or the Koran as fact, thrive with the encouragement of the state.

The atheists have a point: one way or another
it's fair to say that God has had a hefty advantage
over the secular for a very long time. But they must
do two things. They must prove, rather than
merely assert, that mainstream religion is a malign
force in the world. They cannot rely on a small
minority of religious extremists to do that for them
or hark back to the brutality of earlier centuries.
And they must offer an alternative to the millions
who rely on their beliefs to make sense of their
lives.

Unlike the militant atheists I do not think people
are stupid if they believe in God. For vast numbers
of ordinary, thoughtful people it is impossible not
to. Of course, that may be the result of indoctrination at a very early age – but it may also be a
considered reluctance to accept that the material
world is all there is. Quite simply – and this will
cause many an atheist lip to curl – they *want* there
to be something else. That does not mean we
should ignore the argument against it. Some people
can do that. They know what they believe and
that's all there is to it. Most of us, I think, just keep
worrying away at it.

PART ONE

In the Beginning

1

Memories are both gifts and punishments. The first kiss from someone who's not your mother – that sweet little girl in primary school, perhaps – is a gift for sure. But what about the botched attempt at a first snog when teenage hormones have begun to weave their malevolent magic? Undoubtedly a blessing if she feels the same way about you – but a curse if she points out, ever so gently, that of course she likes you, it's just that she doesn't like you in *that* way. Teenage girls can be cruel.

Most memories from childhood swirl around in our consciousness, rub against each other, blend together and, over the years, lose their sharp edges. Most, but not all. Half a century later they can still pierce the treacherous mist of time, sometimes reassuring but often unsettling. I still shudder at the memory of a particular childhood nightmare, still wince at a piece of crass adolescent behaviour as though it had happened just this morning in the *Today* studio, still wonder at the sheer joy when each of my children was born and I held their perfect little bodies for the first time.

And I still recall the exact times and places when the Big Questions declared themselves to my childish consciousness. We all have our own versions of them – with the possible exception of one or two people who probably left the womb knowing all the answers to everything they were ever likely to be asked. But most of them went into politics and spend half their lives dodging questions. The first of my own Big Questions arrived when I was in short trousers and knew even less than I know today.

I had been playing with some friends on a disused aerodrome near my home in Cardiff. The war had ended only a few years earlier but small boys like us were still fighting it every day. Bombed houses were popular battlegrounds – I don't suppose we gave a moment's thought to how close the bombs had fallen to our own homes – but the disused aerodrome was best. We used the abandoned carcasses of old aircraft to attack the squadrons of imaginary German bombers droning above us in the darkening sky. When we had wiped them out, mercifully suffering no casualties of our own, my friends went home for tea. I hung around. It was one of those days when my mother, a hairdresser who worked from home, was giving a perm to a neighbour and I hated the stench of the chemicals.

By now it was dark. Childhood memories of endless, sun-filled summers may be deceptive but childhood memories of star-filled skies are real. The glory of the night sky had yet to be lost to light pollution and on cloudless nights the stars went on for ever. That was what troubled me. How could they go on for ever? And if the universe was everything, what was it all *in*? And how could it be *in* anything because that would have to be in something else and . . . and . . . and so on. And what was there before any of it existed? And how did it all come into existence? And finally – the really, really Big Question – why?

In the old cockpit of my battle-scarred fighter I was worried and slightly scared. Dealing with the worst the Luftwaffe could throw at us had been no problem. Being alone in the 'indifferent immensity of the universe' . . . that was something else. It was an even bigger anxiety than the trouble I'd be in with my mother for being late home for tea.

The other Big Question came to me at about the same age. I was on a bus returning from our week's holiday in Aberystwyth. I hated buses. I was always sick on them and the journey from Cardiff to Aberystwyth on a pre-war bus many years before anyone had thought of motorways was a long one. It was while I was hanging over the platform at the back – banished there by the conductor for obvious reasons – that I discovered mortality. For the first time in my short life I realised that one day I would die.

Once again the question was: why? What was the point of being born if all there was to look forward to was dying? For the length of that ghastly journey and into the next day, everything seemed completely and utterly pointless. Then the normal service of childhood was resumed and it went away. But it came back. Questions like that always do.

It took me a few more years to grasp that rather a lot of people were worrying about their own versions of the Big Questions and had been for quite a long time. The great philosophers and theologians might have framed them in rather more sophisticated terms than that scruffy little boy on a disused aerodrome, but the questions were not so very different.

The seventeenth-century philosopher Blaise Pascal described the predicament of those who do not know why I am set down here rather than elsewhere, nor why the brief period appointed for my life is assigned to me at this moment rather than another in all the eternity that has gone before and will come after me. On all sides I behold nothing but infinity, in which I am a mere atom, a mere passing shadow that returns no more. All I know is that I must die soon, but what I understand least of all is this very death which I cannot escape.

Pascal did not come to believe in a personal God until his early thirties. I was one of the many whose questions were answered by the Church right from the beginning. That served for a while. It was hugely comforting for a small boy to be told that God had made everything, from the most distant galaxy to the tadpoles in your jam-jar – and don't worry about death because if you're good you'll go to heaven. So we could attend church on Sundays and on weekdays get back to fighting the Hun.

There had been no question of my not going to church. That was what we did in my family – all of us except my father, who was almost always either too busy or too tired and did not, I think, believe in God anyway. Not that he'd have dared say so. My mother took the firm view that you were either Christian or you were heathen. And by 'Christian' she meant C of E (or Church of Wales in our case), just like the King. Roman Catholics were viewed with suspicion and non-conformists were simply inferior. The Baptist minister didn't even wear a dog collar, for heaven's sake.

So it was St Saviour's Church in Splott for me, where you called the vicar 'Father', followed the order of service to the letter, would no more have hugged your neighbour than run naked down the aisle, and tried hard not to fall asleep during the sermon, which was, as far as I can remember, pretty much unchanged from week to week.

Most of the time I had only the haziest idea of what was going on. Though I knew every word of the Creed and recited it with as much passion as I could muster, I understood only bits of it. I never did grasp what was meant by the 'quick and the dead'; neither did I know who or what the Holy Ghost was. As for the concept of the Holy Trinity, I still don't understand it. Does *anyone*?

It was inevitable that I would be confirmed, and I took the confirmation classes, with an earnest young curate (whom my father was convinced was homosexual because he was single and once invited a few of us boys to his flat for tea), very seriously. I read the Bible from cover to cover, though I might as well have been reading a telephone directory for all I got out of it. I even created my own prayer book.

I really thought – and fervently hoped – that my confirmation and first communion would have some great transforming effect. How could it not? I was about to eat the body and drink the blood of Our Lord and Saviour Jesus Christ. That was the promise on offer. How could that not transform me? Well, all I know is that it didn't.

If I have any memory of that moment when the wafer was first laid on my crossed hands (for some reason the vicar disapproved of putting it straight on your tongue) and the goblet of wine put to my lips, it was purely sensory: the curious dissolving blandness of the wafer and the slight thrill of being allowed to sip alcohol. I might have felt a little light-headed but I suspect that had more to do with having had to skip breakfast than any spiritual enlightenment. It was to be no different at subsequent communion services.

The words and the solemnity of the Eucharist have stayed with me. Especially that moment when the priest would intone the single sentence that encapsulates the Christian belief:

God so loved the world that he gave his only begotten son, that whosoever believeth in him shall not perish but have everlasting life.

Then, turning his back on the congregation, he would face the altar and raise the goblet of wine above his head. I would join the line of worshippers shuffling slowly up the aisle to the rail trying hard to think only pure thoughts but rarely succeeding.

As the priest talked of drinking the 'blood of the New Covenant, which is shed for many for the remission of sins', my thoughts would usually be on sins I devoutly hoped to be committing before I was very much older. For the present I was concerned with trying to manoeuvre myself into a position so that I knelt between Mary and Marie. Mary was the dark one and Marie the blonde. They were best friends and I think I loved them equally. Love comes easily to a thirteen-year-old boy. But belief?

As I knelt at the rail, waiting for the sacrament, inhaling the cloying incense, trying to focus on the tortured body of Christ on the altar cross rather than the sweet young faces of Mary and Marie, I imagined I believed in God. But I'm not sure that I did. I'm not even sure that a thirteen-year-old boy has the first idea of what it means. Half a century later I'm still not sure.

For a couple of years after I was confirmed I went to church and took communion regularly. At fifteen I left school to work on a local newspaper and then, two years later, left home to work for a bigger paper in the Welsh valleys. It was then that I stopped going to church. I had discovered the joys of jazz concerts and pubs, preferably combined. Saturday night was pub-crawl night, which meant that Sunday morning was spent recovering. But in any case I realised that going to church was a meaningless exercise. I was bored by the ritualised responses, by priests who seemed to have nothing to say, by my own failure to be genuinely moved by any of it.

Yet I continued to pray. I prayed every single night without fail for half a century. In the early days, as I recall, it was pretty selfish stuff and not always in the true spirit of Christian charity. Like the time I prayed for God to kill my headmaster. It wasn't just because I disliked him – though I did – it was because I had been caught, earlier that evening, trespassing on the railway line by a grown-up who said he would report me to my school. Those were the days when punishment was swift and brutal. I knew I'd be called up by the head in the morning and given a whacking, possibly in front of the school. My prayers went unanswered. The head was spared by God but I was not spared by the head.

When I matured a little I developed a pattern of prayer, which I followed every night. I would begin with the Lord's Prayer and one or two others, then ask God's blessing on everyone I could think of who might be in need of help. But I can't say I was any more effective at healing the halt and the lame or helping the needy than I had been at killing off my headmaster. I don't think I ever felt I was really connecting with anything beyond myself.

That's hardly surprising. What I was engaged in was about as far from a conversation with God as if I'd been trying to discuss the state of the economy with my goldfish. It was a mechanical recitation. Only on very rare occasions – usually after something genuinely awful had happened in my own life – did I feel the slightest emotional involvement. And even then it was clearly self-indulgent. So I abandoned the formulaic praying and tried something closer to meditating, tried to empty my mind of the usual daily dross, to 'allow God in', as my old vicar put it. Still nothing.

The problem was that I had absolutely no notion of the God to whom I was supposed to be praying or, for that matter, why I was praying. Did I really think my prayers would make any difference? I doubt it. Their value – if that's the right word – lay in the nightly reminder they provided of how much misery there is in the world. The drawback was that it was obvious they weren't making the slightest difference. Praying seemed to have about as much success in persuading God to end poverty in Africa as I'd been having years before in persuading him to intercede on my behalf with Marie and Mary. So, if I was getting nothing out of it and neither were the people I was praying for, why was I bothering?

There was an element of Hilaire Belloc's instruction to 'always keep a hold of nurse for fear of finding something worse'. I kept praying because I was vaguely afraid to stop. Pathetic, yes, but perhaps no more so than a deathbed conversion. Hedging my bets might be another way to put it. It was also because of those wretched Big Questions. They were still lurking and I clung to the notion that one day enlightenment might result.

Mostly, though, I wanted to believe. I envied friends with an apparently solid faith their certainties and the comfort their faith appeared to bring them. Mostly. I also found some of that certainty occasionally ridiculous and even mildly sinister.

A friend took me to 'HTB', otherwise known as Holy Trinity Brompton, a rich church in the most fashionable area of London. This is where the phenomenally successful 'Alpha Courses' were born. It's the sort of church where you may well be invited to 'give God a clap'. I hated it.

Another friend asked me to attend a Billy Graham meeting in Earl's Court with her. Before we left she told me God helped her in everything she does. Only the other day he had helped her find a screwdriver just when she needed one. I told her the old joke about the Irish Catholic, desperate to find a parking place before a vitally important meeting, who promised God that if he helped out he'd give up smoking, drinking and fornication. Miraculously a place appeared. The Irishman looked up to heaven and said, 'Never mind, I've found one.' My friend was not amused.

On the way to Earl's Court her car broke down. I suggested lightly it must mean God didn't want me to go. No, she said darkly, it's the Devil. She meant it too. But we got to Earl's Court in the end and I watched the great evangelist in action. I had never been to anything like it before. I suppose I was expecting some fiery sermonising that would have the audience quaking in its boots. Instead Dr Graham was as calm and measured as a country vicar talking to the ladies of the flower-arranging committee. He was also – and this may have been because he was tired and feeling his age – surprisingly boring.

There were endless quotations from the Bible to prove whatever point he was making. This always puzzles me: if a preacher is using the Bible to convert someone, to prove that God exists, then surely he must first prove the Bible is the truth and not just a collection of writings that contradict each other and were written long after the events they purport to describe. If, on the other hand, he assumes we already accept the truth of the Bible, why is he trying to convert us?

At the end I stayed in my seat rather than come on up to the front and receive the Lord into my life. Yet again I wasn't quite sure what that meant. Many of those who did 'come on up' looked vaguely embarrassed. You had the feeling they did it because they didn't want to let that nice Dr Graham down. After all, he'd gone to so much trouble. Or perhaps I was still in the grip of the Devil.

I'm uneasy about the evangelical movement. Billy Graham was patently a decent and sincere man and believed every word he spoke, but at its most extreme and pernicious, the movement gives us those dodgy salesmen-preachers who appear on television in the United States and become very rich from persuading the gullible and the vulnerable to hand over to their so-called churches vast amounts of money.

Even at its most benign this version of religion seems to me to offer a false prospectus. There are no ifs, ands or buts about the evangelical message. If you are prepared to accept God into your life, he will come. That's it. And if he doesn't 'come'? Well, by definition, it must be your fault. Everything is black or white. There are no grey areas. That may be fine if you're trying to persuade a three-year-old why he should eat his broccoli, but not so fine when it comes to interpreting what the Bible has to say about how we should lead our lives.

As for the mainstream Anglican Church, it was losing the battle against its own evangelical wing. As I entered my middle age it was haemorrhaging support. The pews were looking emptier Sunday after Sunday. Even its own leaders seemed increasingly unsure about what it was for. They were clearly failing to get across the Christian message and it was hard to resist the conclusion that many were not sure what the message should be and how they should make the Church 'relevant' in a changing world. I wonder if Jesus ever gave much thought to being 'relevant' to his followers.

By now I had pretty much decided to give up on the Church. I kept praying but I also kept wondering why I was doing it. My years as a reporter and foreign correspondent were taking their toll too. There may be no atheists in a foxhole, but there are plenty in the newsroom. Good journalists are – by instinct, experience and training – sceptical. Not cynical but sceptical. If we're not, we're in the wrong job. We're meant to question, to doubt, to challenge.

It is true that the most thoughtful believers ask questions and challenge their own belief. They often struggle to reconcile the merciful, loving God of the Abrahamic religions with the horrors of the world around them. But in the end they succeed. It's either that or lose their faith. I was struggling and failing. Many people experience great tragedy in their lives, but the difference with journalists is that we seek it out. Great tragedies – a sad fact of life – make great stories.

I was a young man, not much more than a boy, when I watched the miners of Aberfan digging for the bodies of their children after the coal tip crushed their school. A few years later when I should have been enjoying Christmas Day with my young family in New York, I was watching weeping mothers trying to free the bodies of their children from the ruins of houses wrecked by an earthquake in Nicaragua.

In various African countries I have seen children, all hope gone from their blank and staring eyes, slowly starving to death. In divided countries all over the world I have seen the bodies of young men horribly mutilated by other young men for no other reason than that they belonged to the wrong tribe or religion.

And in war zones I have listened to soldiers – ordinary people like you and me, with their own children to love and care for – justify the slaughter of other entirely innocent human beings, other children. Perhaps the most common justification is the equivalent of that hideous phrase 'collateral damage'. The school was bombed, the children mown down, the city firebombed because they were in the way. The attack was necessary in pursuit of a greater cause.

And over and over again I was asking myself the other Big Question, one that would not have occurred to the innocent little boy on the aerodrome: where was God? There was, I suppose, a defining moment and it came almost forty years after Aberfan. It was another horror in another school. It was Beslan, but this time it was no hideous accident, no 'act of God'.

On 1 September 2004 a group of armed men took more than a thousand children and teachers hostage. The world watched and prayed for the children. Those prayers were answered not by their safe release but by bloody slaughter. More than 330 people died, among them 176 children.

This was no random, freak event, no desperate stunt that had gone horribly wrong, no moment of insanity by a deranged psychopath. Those men loaded their weapons and laid their explosives in the classrooms in the full, calculating knowledge that they might use them to murder children. Over the three days of the siege they must have come to know many of those children. They must have seen reflected in their frightened young faces the faces of their own children. And yet they butchered them.

Some horrors are on a scale so vast it is impossible to grasp them: the Holocaust, the purges of Stalin, the millions murdered by Mao Tse-tung. But not Beslan. We could grasp it only too well. How many of us imagined our own children in that school, facing that fear?

When the firing stopped I phoned the Archbishop of Canterbury, Dr Rowan Williams, and asked him to come on to *Today* the following morning. I wanted to ask the leader of the Church in which I had grown up and which had promised me endless love and eternal salvation just one question: Where was God in that school? He agreed to talk to me.

That interview led to *Humphrys in Search of God*. In almost half a century of journalism I have never had such a response to anything I have written or broadcast. The letters arrived, quite literally, by the sackful. I had learned a lot from the interviews. I learned even more from the response to them. It felt a bit like putting my fingers on the religious pulse of the nation.

The pulse is still strong. However empty the pews may be in the parish churches on a typical Sunday morning, there are plenty of people with a sincere and passionate belief. That much is evident. There are also plenty of people who think it's all a load of nonsense. But more on that later.

What surprised me is how many think of themselves as neither believers nor atheists but doubters. They, too, are sincere. Devout sceptics, if you like. And many of them feel beleaguered. I'm with them.

So my own spiritual journey – if that's not too high-falutin' a notion – has taken me from my childish Big Questions to my ultimate failure to find any corresponding Big Answers. Along the way I have experienced the indoctrination of confirmation classes, the anticlimax of the Eucharist, the futility of prayer, the contradiction between the promises made by an allegedly merciful, loving God and the reality of a suffering world. So I end up – so far, at any rate – as a doubter.

2

It has taken us some thirteen billion years to get from the Big Bang to where we are today. Our own planet is about 4.6 billion years old. *Homo sapiens* emerged about a hundred thousand years ago. If we convert the time that has passed since the universe came into being into the face of a twenty-four-hour clock, I calculate that humans have been around for 0.024 seconds, give or take a millisecond here or there. Belief in God – the sort of God I'm interested in for the purpose of this book – has existed for an even tinier fraction of that time: a mere 3,800 years or so. However you calculate it, that's not very long.

This strikes me as strange. If, as the three great monotheistic faiths insist, the whole point of God's creation was us – human beings – why did it take him so long to get round to creating us? And once we had finally started running the show on earth, why did it take so much longer to reveal that the main purpose of our existence (the *only* purpose, according to true believers) was to worship him?

Bear in mind that there are only a few more hours left on that twenty-four-hour clock before the end of all life on earth. Awesome pictures captured by the Hubble telescope in early 2007 showed the death throes of a star identical to our own sun. Any planets near it would have been vaporised by the super-hot gases hurtling through space from the explosion. And that is more or less how we shall end in five billion years or so – by which time even *Big Brother* may have run out of 'housemates' prepared to humiliate themselves for our amusement.

That seems a pretty bleak prospect to most of us – and we may well manage that feat even earlier by dint of pumping so much carbon dioxide into the atmosphere that our little planet ends up with no more intelligent life on it than a reality television show. Why did God leave it so late? But I'm getting a bit ahead of myself here. We need to go back to the beginning.

Scientists broadly agree on what happened to make life possible – at least, after the Big Bang. They even think they know how it happened. The first thing to exist was what they call a singularity, which means everything in existence was concentrated into something so small you could put it in your eye and not notice it was there. That's all there was, just this singularity. No space. No light or dark. Nothing except the singularity. It had existed for ever – except that even time didn't exist so I'm not sure how you measure 'for ever'. And just in case you think you may be able to grasp that idea, I should warn you that there are one or two other ideas out there.

A few of the world's more imaginative physicists have come up with the logic-defying notion of 'imaginary' time, which shows (to their satisfaction, at least) that the universe could have been born without a singularity. But let's stay away from that. It's tough enough as it is. Let us instead assume there was such a thing as a singularity and steal Bill Bryson's lovely description of what it did:

> In a single blinding pulse, a moment of glory much too swift and expansive for any form of words, the singularity assumes heavenly directions, space beyond conception.

From then on it was all fairly straightforward – at least, to a physicist. The singularity exploded outwards at a speed that would impress even Jeremy Clarkson. It is still exploding. Distant stars and galaxies are still flying away from each other.

Within a few minutes just about everything that would ever be created had been created.

So, now let's move from the unimaginable and indescribable to what happened next. Compared with the fireworks of the Big Bang this is the relatively boring bit. For brilliant scientists like Martin Rees it is almost prosaic. Lord Rees – Astronomer Royal, president of the Royal Society and much else besides – is one of those who is able to reduce the mysteries of creation to a set of figures. Six numbers, to be precise.

A few decades ago scientists discovered that the stars are actually countless billions of nuclear explosions creating unbelievable amounts of energy. They do it through nuclear fusion, which scientists have been trying to re-create in the laboratory for decades. If they ever crack it, we shall no longer have to worry about drilling for oil or digging coal.

Every element in the universe is made from hydrogen – the simplest and most common of all the elements in the periodic table – created by nuclear fusion in the big stars. For life to exist we need all ninety-odd elements in perfect proportion. The six numbers Rees has come up with prove, to the satisfaction of the small number of physicists who understand these things, that if there had been even the tiniest fluctuation in the force of the explosion there could have been no chemical reaction between the different elements. Life as we know it would not have existed. But everything worked beautifully. The quarks (the smallest particles of all) bunched together to form atoms and the atoms made up the molecules. With enough molecules of the right sort you get living cells. Factor in a few million years of evolution and natural selection and you end up with Beethoven. All it took to get the whole thing going was that one Big Bang.

It may not, of course, have been quite as simple as that – assuming you regard that as simple. The latest theory suggests that there was not one Big Bang in which the whole of time and space was created from nothing, but that our universe was built on the shattered remains of an older universe. The old one was, apparently, similar to ours but collapsed in on itself. The mathematicians who came up with this theory have called it the Big Crunch. Another theory is that there is not one, but a vast number of universes.

Lord Rees is one of many scientists who doubt that the universe has been around long enough to produce the kind of complexity that characterizes the world today. They think there were not enough circumstances, if you like, for change to act on. If it had all come about by chance alone our universe would have had to exist for much longer. So the theory is that there is an infinite number of universes, of which we are one tiny part, and it did not all happen here.

The idea has been with us for a long time, as much a philosophical concept as a scientific one. It has had various names: the multiverse or meta-universe; the parallel universe; quantum universes. They all, apparently, mean much the same thing.

What the theory does most effectively is cut the ground from beneath those who argue for intelligent design. It is tempting to look at the physical laws that enable and determine life and conclude that they are simply too perfect to have come about by accident, but if the theory is right then, as Paul Davies of Arizona State University puts it, our universe has 'hit the jackpot in a gigantic cosmic lottery'. Or maybe it's a variation on monkeys writing the complete works of Shakespeare. They may end up doing it, but they would need an awful lot of time. Davies says:

> The root cause of all the difficulty can be traced
> to the fact that both religion and science appeal

to some agency outside the universe to explain its law-like order. Dumping the problem in the lap of a pre-existing designer is no explanation at all, as it merely begs the question of who designed the designer. But appealing to a host of unseen universes and a set of unexplained meta-laws is scarcely any better.

For those of us without the scientific training of Rees or Davies none of this is terribly helpful. The concepts are simply too strange for us to get our heads round them. I looked for a nice, simple explanation of the multiverse and came up with a Swedish-American cosmologist called Max Tegmark, an associate professor at the Massachusetts Institute of Technology. He has produced a mathematical argument for the multiverse. Allow me to try it out on you:

The computational expression of a single random number between one and zero (with all its infinite decimals) is longer than the computational expression of the whole set of numbers that exist between 1 and 0, so it may be more *informationally economical* for reality to consist of infinite parallel universes instead of just one. The computer code for such a computation is only two lines long.

Does that help? No, I thought not – unless you're a mathematician. But it's impressive, isn't it? It may even be true – so far as it goes. But even though I haven't the foggiest idea what it means, I know what it does not mean. It does not mean that the multiverse exists. It means that clever people with powerful imaginations and even more power-ful computers can produce wonderfully elegant theories of what might be. What they cannot do is produce hard evidence. What they need to come up with is the equivalent of the subtle knife created by Philip Pullman in his wonderful trilogy *His Dark Materials*. Then we could pop out at the weekend, slice a hole in the fabric of our universe, pop into another one and be home in time for tea. Now *that*'s what I call proof.

Instead we have beautiful and bizarre theories of what might be. Or might not be. The supporters of the multiverse theory can rely on many other scientists and mathematicians and cosmologists and physicists who agree with them that this is a very plausible theory indeed. They can argue with huge conviction that the multiverse really must exist – if only because no other theory will do. Many people, without their great knowledge, are persuaded – some because they like the sound of it and many more because they are not satisfied with the theories we already have for why the universe is as it is. They are desperately seeking something else, possibly because they would like to offload some of the responsibility elsewhere for the way we are fouling up this beautiful world of ours. The scientists can't help them. Not that it stops them believing.

Now, what does all this remind you of? What if, instead of 'cosmologists and physicists' we substituted 'priests and theologians' and instead of 'multiverse' we substituted 'God'? Beginning to sound a bit like religion, isn't it? It might even be true. Then again it might not. How would we know? Atheists dismiss with contempt the notion of a creator god. But ask them what happened before the Big Bang and in the end their answers boil down to not much more than 'Dunno really . . . Just happened didn't it? Couldn't have been a creator 'cos something would have had to create the creator . . .' And then it dribbles away as we enter the murky waters of the infinite regress – of which more later.

So much for the physics. So much for the 'what happened'. The next question is: Why? Atheists have no problem with this. They are not required to answer it. If the universe came about by a series of inexplicable coincidences, that's an end to it. If the multiverse theory is true, that's an end to it. Either way, it was an accidental occurrence. Cosmologists might spend their lives trying to prove the theory and 'discovering' another universe but, even if they managed to do that, it would have no bearing on the question of why it happened. It just did.

Religious believers, though, are obliged to come up with an explanation. If there was an intelligent designer, that designer was God. And if God exists, he must have had a reason for doing what he did. C. S. Lewis, one of the most influential Christian thinkers of his time, said the universe must have a meaning for the very obvious reason that if it did not we could never have found out that it did not:

> . . . just as, if there were no light in the universe and therefore no creatures with eyes, we should never know it was dark. Dark would be without meaning.

Convoluted it may be, but you can see his logic. If you accept that it was God who lit the blue touch-paper for the ultimate fireworks display, there are enough questions to keep us going until the next

Big Bang and the biggest of those must be: Why? What was the point of creating us?

I can see – just about – why God would want to do *something*. There wouldn't be much point in just drifting around in space and time – or whatever happened to exist before he created them – engaged in nothing more than the divine equivalent of examining your navel. Equally, there would seem to be little point in going to the trouble of creating something as big and complex as the universe in the full knowledge that it was programmed to destroy itself in a few trillion years – which might seem a long time to you and me but presumably is no more than a blink in God's eternity. What's more, if Earth is the jewel in this celestial crown and its eventual human inhabitants were created in God's image, why turn us into such stroppy, ungrateful, selfish, destructive, warmongering fools, who should not be entrusted with a starter Lego set, let alone a whole planet? Especially when theists tell us the whole point of our existence is to worship that same God.

Theologians, philosophers, biologists and assorted madmen throughout the ages have had their views on all these matters, but let's stay with the scientists for a while longer.

3

People who make their living interviewing other people eventually reach the stage in their careers when they are no longer intimidated by their interviewees, whatever their status and however famous or notorious they may be. Once we have been round the block a few times we tend to take most things in our stride.

It took a while in my case. There have been one or two African dictators who have scared the hell out of me. One locked me up (mercifully briefly) for adopting what he took to be a disrespectful attitude. But he was the epitome of sweet reason compared with Margaret Thatcher. At the height of her power she could do more with a scornful lift of her eyebrow than your average dictator could manage with a dozen Kalashnikov-toting thugs masquerading as bodyguards. I was, frankly, terrified of her.

But she has left the scene and I am no longer the *ingénu*. When prime ministers and presidents are closer in age to your children than they are to you, you lose some of the awe. Even so, I was a bit intimidated by the prospect of interviewing Stephen Hawking – and not just because of the size of his brain.

It was never going to be an easy interview. His disability ensures that. For a start, you can't just turn up and ask questions. You have to email them in advance so that he can type out his answers and enable the synthesiser with the curious voice to do its work. And Hawking is not a man to suffer fools gladly. When a *Guardian* writer, Emma Brockes, sent her questions to him for an interview in 2005 they were returned with a curt note: 'I want shorter, better focused, numbered questions, not a stream of consciousness.' Back to the drawing board, Ms Brockes.

I had that in mind when I turned up for my interview. You expect to meet an eminent Cambridge professor in a book-lined office in an ancient college building steeped in history and mouse droppings. Hawking's office is not like that. It's in a suburb of Cambridge, surrounded by semi-detached houses rather than dreaming spires. This is the Centre for Mathematical Sciences – modern buildings, lots of glass and concrete and, instead of manicured lawns and elegant quadrangles, rather scruffy patches of grass with young men playing football.

His office comes as a surprise too. The humidifier on his desk puffing out steam lends an otherworldly aura to the contents – including the big photo of a young Marilyn Monroe and the little model of Hawking in a wheelchair with a helicopter rotor on top and a boxing glove at the end of an extended arm. It's a memento from his appearance on *The Simpsons*. But the real thing – Stephen Hawking himself – is the biggest surprise.

At first sight he is exactly as you would expect from the thousands of photographs and television appearances – a small, cruelly twisted figure trapped in a wheelchair. But when he looks directly at you it's most unnerving. It seems that he is giving you a beaming smile of welcome – but, of course, he's not. He can't smile. His appalling disease means he can move only one small muscle in his right cheek. Not so much move as twitch. That's the second impression: you think he's winking at you and it's tempting to wink back. It takes you a while to realise that a tiny light is attached to his glasses, shining an infra-red beam on to the computer built into his wheelchair. The twitch breaks the beam and 'clicks' the cursor to select a letter.

Communicating with Stephen Hawking is an incredibly slow and laborious process, but it concentrates the mind wonderfully. You marvel at the sheer bloody-mindedness that must have driven the powerful brain in its pathetic shell of a body to such extraordinary heights. His great achievement was not just to awaken an interest in how the universe works but to have done it on borrowed time. When the motor-neurone disease was diagnosed in his early twenties doctors told Hawking he would be dead in a few years. With chilling understatement he described that as 'a bit of a shock'. For more than forty years he has been proving them wrong.

When I met him in the autumn of 2006 his job was Lucasian Professor of Mathematics at Cambridge, a position once held by Isaac Newton. His biggest book – *A Brief History of Time* – has sold more copies than any other scientific book ever written. It was in the best-selling charts for 237 weeks. Most authors would sell their souls for a month in the charts. It is estimated that about one in every seven hundred people in the world has bought a copy. Sadly, there are no reliable figures for the number of people who have read it from beginning to end – let alone understood it. We may or may not have a vague idea of Einstein's General

Theory of Relativity. We will certainly have heard of Quantum Theory, the other great scientific breakthrough of the first half of the last century. But when it comes to unifying the two and discovering that black holes may not be completely black we begin to wilt. The idea that the universe has no edge or boundary in imaginary time is enough to see most of us off.

But what many of us did understand – or thought we understood – was the last, unforgettable paragraph of his book. It is hard to resist the concept of a 'complete theory of everything', to understand all the laws that govern the existence of the universe. Here's what Hawking wrote about it:

> . . . if we discover a complete theory, it should in time be understandable by everyone, not just by a few scientists. Then we shall all, philosophers, scientists and just ordinary people, be able to take part in the discussion of the question of why it is that we and the universe exist. If we find the answer to that, it would be the ultimate triumph of human reason – for then we should know the mind of God.

When he was reviewing the proofs of the book before publication Hawking considered cutting out that last sentence. He's awfully glad he didn't. He says that if he had, sales of the book might have

halved. Because of those last four words. The very
notion of 'knowing the mind of God' captured the
imagination in a way that a limitless supply of
black holes and dark matter never could. It surprised a lot of people too. Apart from anything
else, isn't this brilliant professor meant to be an
atheist? How could he even entertain the notion of
God, let alone write about knowing his mind?

Believers seized on it. If there really is an answer
to the question of why we and the universe exist,
they said, it can only be because the universe was
created by something outside itself. That 'something' – as Hawking himself acknowledged –
would have to be God. But would it and did
he? Here's what he wrote elsewhere in the book:

> Why does the universe go to all the bother of
> existing? Is the unified theory so compelling that
> it brings about its own existence? Or does it need
> a creator, and, if so, does he have any other effect
> on the universe? And who created him?

That is not Hawking stating a belief; it's Hawking
asking questions. There's a big difference. So I
asked him what he meant. Did he really believe
God was needed to create the universe and, if so,
are we really making any progress towards knowing his mind? Here's how the conversation went:

SH: It seems that the universe is governed by a set of scientific laws. One might say that these laws were the work of God, but it would be an impersonal God, who did not intervene in the universe, apart from setting the laws. What I meant when I said we would know the mind of God, was that if you discovered the complete set of laws, and understood why the universe existed, we would be in the position of God. We are making progress towards that goal, but we still have some way to go. That quest is our greatest challenge.

JH: So this God is no more than (or, if you prefer, no less than) a force of nature. A force of nature that created the entire universe, in one minuscule portion of which we managed to come into existence?

SH: One could define God as the embodiment of the laws of nature. However, this is not what most people would think of as God. They mean a human-like being, with whom one can have a personal relationship. When you look at the vast size of the universe, and how insignificant and accidental human life is in it, that seems most implausible.

So there it is. Stephen Hawking does not believe in anything remotely resembling the personal God of the monotheistic faiths. His 'God', if you can call him that, is the embodiment of the laws of nature. That's pretty much what Albert Einstein thought. Over the years various believers have pored over Einstein's writings for evidence that the greatest scientist of his age shared their faith. He gave them what seemed like encouragement when he said that God 'does not play dice' and when he referred to a 'God who creates and is nature'. But what they really pinned their hopes on was this statement from the great man:

> To sense that behind anything that can be experienced there is a something that our mind cannot grasp and whose beauty and sublimity reaches us only indirectly and as a feeble reflection, this is religiousness. In this sense I am religious.

But Einstein's religion could not have been more different from the theistic religion of Christians, Jews and Muslims. His 'God' is effectively Hawking's God. The philosopher Antony Flew suggested that the conception of God as 'an hypothesized omnipotent, omniscient, incorporeal yet personal Creator' is very different from the

God of Einstein and Hawking. For them, the words 'God' and 'nature' are synonymous. Flew, himself an atheist, wrote:

> If there is a true answer to 'the question of why it is that we and the universe exist' it can only be because, as a matter of fact, the universe was and/or is caused to exist by something outside itself. Even if that is indeed the case it still does not necessarily follow – as is too often and too easily assumed – that such a cause must be a personal God capable of harbouring purposes in creating and sustaining us and the universe which we inhabit.

This is all pretty heady stuff. It may be that scientists like Hawking are right and that, step by step, we shall eventually reach a theory of everything and know the mind of God. It can be safely predicted, though, that you and I will not be around to see it. On the other hand, there are many people who believe they already know the mind of God – that they are in personal touch with him regularly – and they know exactly how everything happened because the Bible tells them. There are also many others who think those people are delusional.

PART TWO
The Battle Lines

4

It is only relatively recently that we have been able to question the existence of God and live to argue another day. Through much of European history it has not been wise to admit to doubt. At best you might find yourself cut off from polite society; at worst you might find yourself dangling from iron hooks in a dank cellar and be cut off in a more literal sense. That changed with the European Enlightenment and the dawn of rational debate – though we remained an overwhelmingly God-fearing people.

With the end of the Victorian era the British began to enter an age of religious apathy and after the Second World War religious observance was really going out of fashion. By the time the satirists appeared on the scene in the sixties, the churches were getting worried. Alan Bennett's well-meaning vicar with his vacuous sermons caught the national attitude perfectly:

Life, you know, is rather like opening a tin of sardines. We all of us are looking for the key. And I wonder how many of you here tonight have wasted years of your lives looking behind the kitchen dressers of this life for that key. I know I have. Others think they've found the key, don't they? They roll back the lid of the sardine tin of life. They reveal the sardines – the riches of life – therein, and they get them out, and they enjoy them. But, you know, there's always a little bit in the corner you can't get out. I wonder is there a little bit in the corner of your life? I know there is in mine!

Wickedly funny, but all good-natured stuff. More and more of us were coming to view the Church with an amused tolerance. Those who stayed in bed on Sunday mornings were perfectly happy if others went to church, just so long as no one tried to persuade them to join in. But for some years now there have been growing signs that we are embarking on another religious age. We might, perhaps, call it the age of intolerance. Apathy is giving way to outright hostilities.

Over the last couple of decades evangelicals in the Church of England have declared war on wishy-washy vicars with no fire in their souls, intellectuals who refuse to accept the literal word of the Gospels and liberals who tolerate women priests and, God forbid, homosexuality. It was no wonder, they said, that the faithful were turning their backs on religion when the Church itself seemed no longer to believe in anything.

The last straw (of many) was that the Bishop of Durham, David Jenkins, the third most senior bishop in the Church, cast doubt on the literal nature of Christ's resurrection and used the expression 'a conjuring trick with bones'. I talked about that at length with him for a BBC2 programme and he insisted he had never used those words to describe the resurrection. On the contrary, he had said the resurrection was *more than* a conjuring trick with bones. But the damage was done and, anyway, there was no disguising the theological chasm between a liberal like Jenkins and supporters of the charismatic happy-clappy wing.

The charismatics were determined to regain lost ground and they have done pretty well, winning many converts to their version of robust Christianity. But in the last few years some of the most high-profile atheists at the opposite end of the spectrum have staged their own 'revival'. They have abandoned their amused disdain and taken

IN GOD WE DOUBT

the fight to the enemy. It's getting pretty bloody. Just as the worst wars are civil wars, so the nastiest arguments are those within families. The academic family is particularly disputatious.

Professors at our ancient universities may have brains the size of Antarctica and enough qualifications to cover the ice sheet, but when they quarrel it is not unlike watching a couple of small boys fighting over who got the biggest slice of cake at the birthday party. It may start out on a rarefied intellectual level but it often descends quickly to a slanging match.

Normally this sort of thing can be safely ignored by those of us who have to get on with life in the real world. The chances are anyway that what they are arguing about often has no more relevance to us than earnest debate about the sex of angels or how many can dance together on the head of a pin. But the quarrel about God that has been engaging some of our most eminent dons is real and important.

William Lane Craig is an American evangelical academic who got one PhD from Birmingham University, another from Munich, is now Research Professor of Philosophy at a theological college in California and has built up a considerable reputation among Christian activists around the world as a robust defender of their faith. He believes that a battle is being fought on our campuses for young hearts and minds:

> The average Christian does not realise there is an intellectual war going on in the universities and in the professional journals and scholarly societies. Christianity is being attacked from all sides as irrational or outmoded and millions of students, our future generations of leaders, have absorbed this viewpoint. This is a war which we cannot afford to lose.

As for the churches, Craig thinks they are filled with Christians who are 'idling in intellectual neutral . . . as Christians their minds are going to waste'. If Christian laymen don't become intellectually engaged, he says, then 'we are in serious danger of losing our children'.

Professor Craig, as you will have gathered, is not a man given to understatement. He is a curious mixture of tub-thumping zealot and rational philosopher. When I suggested to him that he presents himself as a sort of intellectuals' Billy Graham he seemed pleased with the description. If you spotted him walking up your garden path one Sunday morning in his neatly buttoned blazer and striped tie, clutching a Bible and smiling in that way evangelicals seem to have made their own, you'd probably hide in the living room and pretend not to hear the doorbell. But that might prove a mistake if you enjoy a good argument. He is clever and knowledgeable. He may not be a barrel of laughs, but I suppose if you're fighting a war against the Anti-christ, a sense of humour is not an essential weapon. Especially if your enemy is Richard Dawkins.

Dawkins has become the most famous atheist in Britain, which may be one of the reasons why he is vilified by so many of his distinguished colleagues. I mean for his fame as well as his atheism. There is a tendency in the groves of academe to subscribe to the view expressed by Gore Vidal: 'Whenever a friend succeeds, a little something in me dies.' Dawkins has succeeded beyond the wildest dreams of most of his academic friends and colleagues. It doesn't help that he is handsome, charming and married to a lovely actress. He might just have got away with that had he not also been voted one of the world's top three intellectuals by the readers of *Prospect* magazine – which was probably enough in itself to win their undying envy. But worse – much worse – than all of that, he has sold more books than most of his fellow professors put together.

When he wrote *The Selfish Gene* it was widely regarded as the finest account of how Darwin's theory of natural selection works. It sold shedloads. So did *The God Delusion*, one of the mostly unlikely best-sellers of the past few years. It might not have threatened *Harry Potter* in the charts, but for a serious book on a serious subject it justified the overused description 'a publishing phenomenon'.

All this would, as I say, have been bad enough, but Dawkins has dominated the columns of high-brow newspapers and magazines and – to add insult to already grievous injury – has even had to himself a whole television programme in which to expound his views. All in all, it amounts to unforgivable behaviour in the eyes of many colleagues.

A fellow Oxford don, Professor Alister McGrath, was one of those who took the battle to him using the academics' weapon of choice: another book. In answer to *The God Delusion* McGrath produced *The Dawkins Delusion*. Dawkins is Professor for the Public Understanding of Science at Oxford and regards theology as a bogus discipline. McGrath is Professor of Historical Theology at Oxford University.

As a young man McGrath was 'passionately and totally' persuaded of the truth and relevance of atheism. He grew up in Northern Ireland and blamed religion for the terrible problems that were tearing the province apart. Then, when he went to Oxford as a student, he encountered something he had failed to meet at home: 'articulate Christians who were able to challenge my atheism'.

He holds a doctorate in molecular biophysics but switched to theology when he discovered that 'Christianity actually worked: it brought purpose and dignity to life.' He became persuaded that Christianity was a 'much more interesting and intellectually exciting world view than atheism'. So his intellectual journey has been precisely the opposite from that of his fellow don Richard Dawkins.

With just the merest hint of sarcasm, McGrath attributes to Dawkins two possible explanations for why the two men could have drawn such different conclusions on the basis of reflecting long and hard on substantially the same world. Here's one:

Because I believe in God, I am deranged, deluded, deceived and deceiving, my intellectual capacity having been warped through having been hijacked by an infectious, malignant God-virus.

And here is the other:

Because I am deranged, deluded, deceived and deceiving, my intellectual capacity having been warped through having been hijacked by an infectious, malignant God-virus, I believe in God.

McGrath sets up those two 'explanations' in order to knock them down. He accuses Dawkins of 'ridiculous nonsense' and he professes himself appalled that Dawkins characterises people like him in such a way. He accuses him of offering

. . . the atheist equivalent of slick hellfire preaching, substituting turbocharged rhetoric and highly selective manipulation of facts for careful, evidence-based thinking . . . the approach of a non-thinking dogmatist.

The truth is, there's a lot of dogmatism in books about religion on both sides of the divide, but to call Dawkins non-thinking is a bit below the belt. Whether he will succeed in his ultimate aim is doubtful, though. There may well be some waverers who will be impressed by his writing and the sheer force of his argument and will opt for the Dawkins brand of atheism, but I doubt many believers will say, 'Dammit! Dawkins is right and my Bible's going in the bin.'

For that to happen there would have to be a different foundation for their faith. Most have not come to it through a process of argument or even rational thinking. It is much more likely to be intuitive, instinctive, visceral, emotional. Or it may be the result of indoctrination, upbringing or environment. Or it may have been born of a specific personal experience or a 'revelation' – a Damascene conversion. Or there may have been a dozen other factors, almost all of which will have had a lot more to do with hearts than with minds.

In simple terms, they believe because they believe. This applies as much to the humble peasant, who may never have read a book in his life and would no more dream of questioning what he is told by his priest than he would try to sow his seeds in the snows of midwinter, as to some of the most educated and sophisticated thinkers of the age.

Dr Rowan Williams, the Archbishop of Canterbury, comes into the category of sophisticated thinker. Indeed, one of the criticisms often levelled at him – and archbishops always come in for plenty of stick – is that he's too clever by half. There's something in that. Unless you speak the academic's special language, you need a steady supply of cold towels to wrap round your head when you read his writings. But they are worth the effort. He has a lot to say.

Williams was a leading academic theologian for many years and was appointed to head the Anglican Church partly on the basis of his piety and patent sincerity, but also because he was deemed intellectually robust enough to stand up to the fiercest buffeting from the likes of Dawkins or Lewis Wolpert, Professor of Biology at University College London. Yet note what the archbishop says about belief. I spoke to him for my Radio 4 series and we argued at length about whether it is possible to *know* there is a God or merely to *believe* it. Intriguingly for a man who made his religious reputation studying and teaching theology, he seems impatient with people who seek God through reason and argument – or even through emotion. Here's what he said in a sermon before he became archbishop:

> If you want God, then you must be prepared to let go of all – absolutely all – substitute satisfac-

tions, intellectual and emotional. You must recognise that God is so unlike whatever can be
thought or pictured that, when you have got
beyond the stage of self-indulgent religiosity,
there will be nothing you can securely know
or feel. You face a blank and any attempt to
avoid that or shy away from it is a return to
playing comfortable religious games . . . If you
genuinely desire union with the unspeakable love
of God, then you must be prepared to have your
'religious' world shattered. If you think devo-
tional practices, theological insights, even charitable actions give you some sort of purchase on
God, you are still playing games.

In our interview I put the question to him
directly. Did he *know* there is a God or *believe*
it? Here's what he said:

I don't know that there is God or a God in the
simple sense that I can tick that off as an item I'm
familiar with. Believing is a matter of being
committed to the reality of God: the knowledge
that comes, that grows if you like, through a
relationship. I believe I commit myself. I accept
what God gives me . . . Grow in that relationship and you grow in a kind of certainty or
anchorage in the belief. Knowledge? Well, yes

– of a certain kind – but not acquaintance with a particular fact or a particular state of affairs. It's the knowledge that comes from relation and takes time.

The point, surely, is that once someone believes something – whether it is a religious faith or something quite different – it is very difficult to shake their belief. That need not mean (though sometimes it will) that the believer is stupid or unthinking. Lewis Wolpert describes a study in which students who were either for or against capital punishment were shown the result of recent studies on the subject. The result of one study confirmed their existing beliefs and the other challenged them. Both groups accepted only the study that confirmed what they thought.

What this shows is that most of us want our beliefs to be confirmed rather than proved false, and we will disregard any inconvenient evidence. And that, as I say, seems to apply no matter how clever you are. Sigmund Freud once said:

To begin with it was only tentatively that I put forward the views that I had developed . . . but in the course of time they gained such a hold of me that I can no longer think in any other way.

79

Our beliefs become a part of who and what we are.

Wolpert tells the story of a scientist who visited the offices of Niels Bohr, one of the world's great physicists and winner of the Nobel Prize for his work. The scientist, says Wolpert, was amazed to find a horseshoe nailed to the wall over the great man's desk. 'Surely,' he asked Bohr, 'you don't believe that horseshoe will bring you luck?' Bohr replied:

'I believe no such thing, my good friend. Not at all. I am scarcely likely to believe in such foolish nonsense. However, I am told that a horseshoe will bring you good luck whether you believe in it or not!'

I'm not quite sure whether it is possible to be both funny and profound in the same breath. If it is, then Bohr deserves another Nobel for that answer.

Lewis Wolpert is a Jew who lost his faith when he was about sixteen. He had said his prayers every night and asked God for help on various occasions but, as he puts it, 'It did not seem to help.' So he gave it up. He is now what he calls a 'reductionist materialistic atheist'. Unlike Dawkins he does not set out to disparage the views of those who believe. His own son Matthew is a believer. Matthew had been through a difficult late adolescence and joined the London Church of Christ, a fundamental Christian church that takes the Bible literally. His friends assumed Wolpert would be upset, but he was not because the Church helped Matthew. And then one day he had an unsettling conversation with him.

> Sitting in my office, Matthew said he was so envious of me, as I was so fortunate. Unused to receiving such a positive remark from any of my children, I beamed and asked what he so envied. The reply was: 'You are going to die soon, certainly before me.'

Wolpert was shocked. The reason Matthew wanted to die was so that he could go to heaven but, of course, according to his religious rules, he could not take his life. Wolpert tells that story in his latest book, whose title is taken from what the Queen instructed Alice she should be prepared to believe in *Through the Looking-Glass*. It is called *Six Impossible Things Before Breakfast*. That sums up the atheist view nicely.

William Lane Craig, of course, believes every one of those 'impossible' things. I wanted to know what happens when you bring together someone with his views and someone like Wolpert, so I agreed to chair a debate between them at Westminster Central Hall in London.

5

Over the years I have chaired enough conferences and public meetings to know how difficult it is to get a decent crowd for a debate. You can tell the difference between amateurs and professionals in the business of organising events. The amateurs always put out a few extra chairs – in case the crowd is bigger than they'd expected. 'It wouldn't do to force anyone to stand, would it?' they ask anxiously, as you stand in the wings peering out at row after row of empty seats, a few dozen lonely people hunkered down at the back so far from the stage you need semaphore to make contact.

Professionals, especially political-party organisers, do exactly the opposite. They put out fewer chairs in the hall than they think they will need. What matters is filling every one. A small, crowded hall always looks better to the cameras than a half-empty bigger one, even if there are more people in it. And if a few people are forced to stand at the back, that's even better. The pro knows that half of those who say they will turn up probably won't bother, especially if they haven't had to pay for their tickets.

Admittedly it's different if you have a very, very big name on the stage. Bill Clinton perhaps. Or Hillary. But William Lane Craig? I'm prepared to bet that many of you had never heard of him until you read this. And yet, on a wet and windy winter's night, he filled Westminster Central Hall in London. And it's a big hall: more than two thousand seats.

When I say *he* filled it I'm being a little unkind to the other speaker, Lewis Wolpert. Professor Wolpert has no trouble filling a lecture theatre at his university, but he's a modest man and would be the first to admit that he would struggle to draw a crowd of well over two thousand. No, it was Professor Craig who did it – with a little help from God. I can say that with confidence because I asked the audience to put up their hands if they believed in God. All but a tiny handful – maybe five per cent – did so. The evangelical network is impressive. Wolpert knew he was beaten before he got to his feet.

At first blush Craig's approach is a million miles away from the evangelical rhetoric of the hellfire-and-brimstone preachers of whom there are so many in the United States. Or, indeed, from that of his fellow Americans who are proud to call themselves creationists – as many as 53 per cent, if a Gallup Poll is to be believed. A tenth of all American religious colleges teach the literal truth of the Book of Genesis, which tells us that God created the world six thousand years ago. That, as the American philosopher and neuroscientist Sam Smith points out, is about a thousand years after the Sumerians invented glue.

If Genesis is right, we should dump Darwin in the bin with all that stuff about fossils and fancy scientific techniques such as dating of the ice core. Don't believe the rubbish about dinosaurs roaming the planet 150 million years ago. If it's only a few thousand years since the divine creation of every kind of plant and creature, it follows that they could not have. My youngest child, possibly one of the world's leading experts on dinosaurs at the age of six, will have some rethinking to do. But if the Bible is the literal word of God, that's that. He'll have to get used to it.

Perhaps I should take him to a new museum in Kentucky that is dedicated to exploring the history of the earth in a somewhat unconventional way. There are, as you might expect, plenty of models of dinosaurs – not unlike those in the Natural History

Museum in London. The difference is that they roam the Garden of Eden alongside Adam and Eve, living in peaceful harmony with them as they nibble the leaves from the trees. Quite sweet, really. It cost $27 million to build.

Well, you don't get that particular brand of tosh from Professor Craig. He is careful to draw a distinction between 'young world creationists' – of whom he disapproves – and 'creationists' of whom he is one. His approach, he says, is based on reason and logic, not blind faith in a mysterious God. He even spends a great deal of time and effort explaining why the Big Bang is the only credible theory of how everything came into existence.

Given this, you might assume that an encounter between someone like Craig and someone like Wolpert would produce riveting intellectual knockabout at least and a profound discussion of whether God is delusion or reality at best. That was what I expected. Sadly, it did not work out like that. The two men might as well have been on different planets.

Here is the essence of the case presented by Craig:

- God created the universe. The proof lies in the premise that whatever begins to exist has a cause. The universe began to exist; therefore it has a cause. It was brought into existence by something that is greater than (and beyond) it. And that something was a 'personal being'.

- God 'fine tunes' the universe for ever. There is no other logical explanation for the way things operate.
- Without God there can be no set of moral values.
- The 'historical facts' of the life of Jesus prove the basis for Christianity.
- God can be known and experienced.

And here is the essence of Wolpert's rebuttal:

- It's bunkum.
- All of it.

Of course he had more to say than that and he said it with some wit, if with a sense of growing weariness. But how can an atheist genuinely engage intellectually with a believer? They face an impossible barrier before they begin. This has nothing to do with detailed textual analysis of the scriptures, or agonising over the precise meaning of the Trinity and the Holy Spirit. It doesn't even have anything to do with bizarre claims made by a Hollywood film director and his ancient ossuaries. It has to do with the origin of the universe and this question:

If God created the universe, what created God?

That is the question to which Wolpert and all atheists return time and again. In the language employed by Dawkins:

Any God capable of designing anything would have to be complex enough to demand the same kind of explanation in his own right.

In other words, if someone *were* able to provide the explanation, we would be forced to embark upon what philosophers call an infinite regress. Having established who created God, we would then have to answer the question of who created God's creator. But it could not end there. We would have to find out who created *him*. And so on *ad infinitum*.

But Craig and his followers dismiss the conundrum. It is not only impossible to answer the question, he says, it is ridiculous even to ask it. And the reason for that is obvious. Nothing could have created God. God existed before time.

Moving for a moment from the profound to the absurd I can't help recalling a conversation between God and Man in that masterpiece of clever nonsense by Douglas Adams, *The Hitchhiker's Guide to the Galaxy.*

'I refuse to prove that I exist,' says God, 'for proof denies faith and without faith I am nothing.'

'Oh,' says Man, 'but the Babel Fish is a dead give-away, isn't it? It proves you exist, and so therefore you don't. Q.E.D.'

'Oh, I hadn't thought of that,' says God, who promptly vanishes in a puff of logic.

Ah, you might say, if only it were that simple. Well, in a way it is. If you accept Craig's answer to the creation question, everything follows. It is possible to buy the whole package. If you don't, none of it follows. When you open the package and discard the wrapping-paper and the box, there is nothing left.

But what explanation does Wolpert have for the creation of the universe? He doesn't know and he's not in the least ashamed to admit it. Craig insisted during the debate that it was up to Wolpert to prove that God is an illusion. Wolpert insisted it was the other way round. He did not, alas, have the Babel Fish at hand to make his point. But he did have a logical platform on which to stand and it's one that all of us with children can recognise.

Most parents use various means of deception when their children are young to persuade them that Father Christmas and the tooth fairy exist. When they are very small the children are more than happy to accept the evidence of the stocking full of toys at the end of the bed or the tooth replaced by a coin slipped under their pillow. But when they grow older the standard of proof becomes more demanding. We might get away with it for a while – after all, they *want* to believe – but sooner or later the precocious little sceptics will tell us the evidence is bogus and, anyway, they stayed awake and saw us put the stocking at the end of the bed. It's not much good at that point demanding that they *prove* Father Christmas doesn't exist.

Instead of Douglas Adams and his weird and wonderful creations, atheists such as Wolpert and Dawkins are fond of quoting the twentieth-century philosopher Bertrand Russell, who came up with a somewhat weird creation of his own: an extra-terrestrial teapot. Russell believed it was incumbent on dogmatists to prove received dogmas rather than the other way round.

He illustrated this by imagining that between Earth and Mars a china teapot revolves about the sun in an elliptical orbit. If he claimed that it was too small to be seen even by the most powerful telescopes, he said, nobody would be able to disprove it. But he added:

> . . . If I were to go on to say that, since my assertion cannot be disproved, it is intolerable presumption on the part of human reason to doubt it, I should rightly be thought to be talking nonsense.

So far so obvious. But Russell goes on to say that if the existence of the teapot were written about in ancient books and 'taught as the sacred truth every Sunday, and instilled into the minds of children at school', the picture changes. Then, he says, if people were reluctant to believe it their hesitation 'would become a mark of eccentricity'.

That's all very well, but the fact is that the existence of an orbiting china teapot has *not* been instilled into the minds of our children and the existence of God has. And religion has survived throughout the millennia in a way that the 'teapot doctrine' is unlikely to do – and, no, Professor Russell, I can't actually prove that claim in any way that might satisfy your rigorous standard of logic. Just call it a hunch.

Douglas Adams might not have scaled the academic heights in the way that Bertrand Russell did, but he was an impressive man. I knew him well enough to recognise that he was deeply serious as well as very funny, creative and more than capable of giving plenty of philosophers a run for their money. That absurd conversation between God and Man made as much sense as Russell's teapot. When he put those words into God's mouth – 'I refuse to prove that I exist for proof denies faith and without faith I am nothing' – he got to the essence of religion.

When Wolpert stood on that platform in Westminster Central Hall and faced that sea of mostly young faces, almost all of whose owners believed in God, he knew he had no chance of changing their minds. Neither, he told them, did he particularly want to. Unlike Dawkins, for whom religion is not only stupid but dangerous, Wolpert believes it is not such a bad thing. That, he says, is because it makes so many people feel better about life. And that, in turn, is why so many people believe. Wolpert says the propensity to believe is in our genes. None of it has anything to do with the existence of God.

Wolpert is a brilliant biologist. Keith Ward is regarded by his peers as a brilliant theologian. He believes that God created the universe but he knows perfectly well that it's impossible to prove it. Neither does he think religion is meant to explain things. Science, he says, is meant to do that:

> Aristotle and Plato had science – but religion is something different. Religion is not about explaining things. Religion is about coming to terms with human existence – facing suffering and death, purpose and values. These are the things religions are concerned with and you don't get 'explanations' . . . It's a bit like saying, if you fall in love with someone and marry them and you say, 'What does she explain?', the answer probably is: she doesn't explain anything! But she's transformed my life and the whole thing seems different because of this relationship.

So let us take Ward at his word: religion does not have to explain how God came to create the world. But he wants us to accept that religion is about coming to terms with human existence. Surely, then, we are entitled to ask what is the point of human existence and why God chose to create humans. If we fall in love and marry it's because we believe we will find happiness, that we'll be more complete as a couple than as two separate individuals. Why would God go to the trouble of inventing the universe and populating this world with human beings when he was already, to use Ward's own description, 'perfect in self-knowing and self-willing'? This is how Ward answers it – and bear in mind as you read this that he is an academic delivering a lecture:

> The reason God should actualise such beings [that means us] is normally thought to be that it is good to do so. Such created beings can enjoy something of the enjoyment that God derives from knowing and willing, and so they increase the number of beings who enjoy, which is good. Perhaps, too, God can enjoy different sorts of actualities by co-operating and sharing experiences with such created personal beings. On some Christian interpretations, it is part of the divine nature to be essentially loving, which involves some form of relationship to other persons, and therefore some creation of such persons. Whether or not that is so, created persons are in the Jewish and Christian traditions said to be like God in having knowledge and will, though their knowing and willing is limited in a way that God's is not.

Putting aside knowledge and will, if we are like God in that respect why do we need physical bodies as well – with all the problems and physical defects that cause such misery and suffering? Why can't we just drift around some infinite cosmos as disembodied spirits, presumably in the same way that God drifts around? Couldn't we be like plankton in the vast ocean of the universe? Why, as Ward puts it, are we 'physical organisms, animals with 46 chromosomes and a particular genome, composed of quarks and leptons'? Here's his answer.

> One possibility is that human agents are emergent parts of a developing cosmos, which generates within itself creative communities of conscious agents. One intelligible purpose for creating a universe like this could be to generate relatively autonomous materially embodied agents which come to understand their own structure and to direct their own future, by the co-operative action of communities of personal beings which are generated within the cosmos from its own inherent potentialities.

Is that clear to you? If not, I suspect you're in good company. The thing that worries me about this sort of explanation (quite apart from its sheer complexity) is that it doesn't actually explain very much at all. What you tend to be left with after the 'may be' and 'could be' and 'seems to be' and 'perhaps' qualifications, is an hypothesis that cannot be proved. Not now. Not ever. I could offer a conjecture that God really is an old man with a long beard floating on a cloud surrounded by angels (which is what some children believe, after all) or that the entire universe is just a vast computer game he created for his own entertainment. Maybe *The Matrix* wasn't such a barmy film. But I can't prove any of that.

We might just as well accept the explanation of a biologist like Stephen J. Gould. At least it has the benefit of being so simple that even those of us who have not been trained as philosophers or theologians can understand it. Gould argues that humanity is an accident. People came about as a result of a freak event. If we ran through the evolutionary process again it would come out quite differently and human beings would probably not emerge. There is so much sheer chance in evolution, so many random mutations and environmental catastrophes, that it is amazing any complex conscious beings evolved. If some disaster had not wiped out the dinosaurs, humans would almost certainly never have existed. So, as Ward paraphrases Gould, 'We owe our existence to an accidental disaster, perhaps an asteroid hitting the earth, and not to any careful plan.'

Of course, clever Christians like Ward accept that we may never be able to eliminate the 'accidental and historical elements' from our understanding of nature:

> Because we can never get a precise enough grasp of the initial conditions of any process, and because of the limitations placed by quantum theory upon our knowledge of all the properties of physical objects, many events will seem to us to be accidents, things that could very easily have been otherwise. But could they really have been otherwise?

This is where it all becomes gloriously tangled. Remember that theists (Jews, Christians, Muslims) not only believe that God created the universe and everything in it, but that he is omnipotent. He makes the laws that determine how everything works – whether it's the evolution of a blob into a human or the ultimate death of the sun. Scientists who do not believe in God say that, yes, of course there are physical laws that determine the way the universe works but they just happened to come into existence for reasons we have yet to understand. Many believers say God could break every 'law' of nature because he created them. So they're not really 'laws' at all. They are just what God determines at any given point. That is not what Ward believes, but neither does he accept that every physical state is determined by the laws of nature operating on previous physical states.

> If the universe was run through again, a determinist must think that exactly the same things would happen again. Now if God set the universe up, it will be utterly obvious to God, and completely determined at the first moment of creation, what will happen throughout the process. Far from being a hazardous process, subject to all sorts of possible accidents, the history of the universe will be predetermined in all its details. So it may be that the process has been set up as a simple initial state plus a set of elegant general laws, so as to result inevitably in the existence of communities of rational agents and the values they embody. The existence of human beings will not be a freak accident at all.

This kind of argument has kept the world's cleverest academics going for centuries and will do so for centuries to come. For most ordinary people who are trying to decide whether God exists it's about as useful as a textbook on quantum mechanics to a child who hasn't yet learned to read. That's not to say we are stupid, just that most of us don't think like theologians.

On the morning of the Westminster Central Hall debate I had spent two hours talking to William Lane Craig across my kitchen table. There were times when I felt like banging my head on it – it may not have done me any harm if I had. I *think* we agreed the existence of the table could be proved but I'm not absolutely certain that we did. He wouldn't say he was 100 per cent certain about it.

Suppose a brain in a vat of chemicals were being stimulated by a mad scientist with electrodes to think there's an external world. My experiences of this table would be the same . . . but I'm not so sure I would say with 100 per cent certainty that I know it.

So, in that vein, I asked him the same question I had asked the Archbishop of Canterbury: did he know God existed or did he merely believe it? He said:

Very often people associate proof with a 100 per cent certainty or a mathematical certainty and

I'm not claiming that. By proof what I would mean would be a cogent argument and a cogent argument philosophically would be an argument that is logically valid. It has true premises and the premises are more plausible than their contra-dictories. And if you have those elements then I think there are good arguments for the existence of God.

Fine, but if you style yourself, as he does, a 'Christian philosopher who is an activist as a Christian', aren't you bound to find the arguments for God 'logical'? Isn't it a question of beginning with the conclusion and working back from it, finding the evidence to support something you've already decided on? Doesn't everything flow from your belief?

And then there's the other question that Pro-fessor Ward set out to answer: Why? Why did God bother to create the universe? Craig's answer, when you've boiled everything else away, was much simpler. He did it for our benefit.

This strikes me as strange for many reasons, not least because so many people lead hellish lives. But apparently that's not the point. The point is that we are all going to experience the infinite love and mercy of God if we are prepared to accept him.

Just as Craig has done. And that's the nub of it, isn't it?

At the end of the debate I asked him this question. Assuming (big assumption, I know) that Lewis Wolpert had been able to demolish his arguments, would that have destroyed his faith? His answer was no. That had to be his answer. If faith can be proved, it's not faith. I *know* that table exists; I don't *believe* it.

How had he come by his faith in the first place? He'd found a girl. He'd 'begun to ask the big questions in life' and didn't find any answers in his church. And then one day,

> I sat behind this radiant, happy person. She was so happy all the time it just made me sick. And I asked her one day what she was so happy about and she said, 'It's because I know Jesus Christ is my personal saviour.' Then she told me: 'He loves you, Bill' . . . I had never heard that before and it just overwhelmed me.

So here is this man who can quote at length every philosopher you have ever heard of and (in my case) many you haven't. A man who analyses their arguments in detail. A man who talks about cosmology and quantum mechanics with the ease of an expert in the field. A man who seems

genuinely to believe that his arguments prove the
existence of God and who wants every Christian
student in the land to get out there and fight the
good fight with all their might. And he turns out to
have come to it because of a smiling girl who sat in
front of him during a German lesson thirty years
ago.

No wonder Lewis Wolpert couldn't get a grip
on him. You cannot argue with the allure of a
smiling girl.

For the record, incidentally, there was another
debate at Westminster Central Hall a few months
after the one I chaired. It pitched atheists (Dawkins, Grayling and Hitchens) against three equally
clever believers (the archaeologist Nigel Spivey,
Rabbi Julia Neuberger and Professor Roger Scru-
ton). Once again the huge hall was crowded – but
this time not with believers. The motion was
'We'd be better off without religion.' Before the
debate began they took a vote. It was 826 for the
motion; 681 against; 364 don't-knows. When it
ended the vote was 1,205 for and 778 against.

6

I began this section of the book with the Big Bang and the Big Questions. Did God create the universe and everything in it? Did he light the blue touch-paper to make life possible and, if so, why? The only possible answer based on anything that could be described even remotely as evidence is: we don't know. It cannot be said too often: there is no way of proving what happened before the moment of creation – assuming there *was* a moment of creation – because there was no space and there was no time. So let's deal with what we do know about: the existence of religion.

We can be reasonably certain that human beings have always wanted to turn to some power greater than themselves. If not the sun, perhaps the moon or fire or the earth itself. Archaeologists have found evidence that Neolithic man worshipped various goddesses in the form of birds and bears. The ancient Egyptians were pretty impressed by cats and the ancient Romans had more gods than orgies.

Throughout history and prehistory animists of one sort or another have believed that body and soul are literally inseparable and that plants, animals and even objects have souls. We may scoff at some of the more bizarre beliefs of our prehistoric ancestors but let us not forget that every age – indeed, every generation – produces its own cults and religions.

To take just one example from today: seemingly intelligent people describe themselves as Scientologists and some countries even accept Scientology as a religion. It makes sense, as far as I can tell, only if you are prepared to believe that thetans (souls, to you and me) have been around for trillions of years. That happens to be several orders of magnitude longer than the universe has been in existence. Sadly, I can't divulge the greatest truths about Scientology because it takes an awfully long time (not to mention pretty deep pockets) to go through the various levels. But I do know, because their website says so, that once you become an 'operating thetan' you are able to

. . . handle things without having to use a body of physical means. Basically one is oneself, can handle things and exist without physical support and assistance.

Now that really could come in very handy indeed – especially the bit about existing without physical support. I wonder if they know that in Darfur or Zimbabwe.

The 'Church' gets a little cross about some of the stories that leak out. There's the intriguing business of Xenu, for instance, an alien ruler of the 'Galactic Confederacy'. It appears that seventy-five million years ago he brought billions of people to Earth in a spacecraft and blew them up with hydrogen bombs. Their souls then clustered together and stuck to the bodies of the living. The alien souls continue to do this today, causing a variety of physical problems in modern-day humans. The trick, it seems, is to isolate them and neutralise the ill-effects. I have every confidence that Tom Cruise will be able to deal with that little problem. Look how good he was in *Top Gun*.

It's easy to scoff at this sort of nonsense (not that we should necessarily resist the temptation) but is it any sillier than the belief among a group of people who live in the South Pacific that Prince Philip is a god? And what about the 'cargo cults' of Pacific Melanesia and New Guinea? David Attenborough, who studies people as well as animals, has written about them. They've been around ever since white men first landed on the islands in the nineteenth century.

The cults are so named because the locals were baffled by the fact that the strangers had all sorts of wonderful gadgets which they never made themselves. When they broke down or needed replacing, new ones arrived in ships or planes. All the natives ever saw the white men do was sit at desks scribbling on paper. They concluded that the writing was some sort of religious devotion and the 'cargo' was of supernatural origin. Richard Dawkins makes the point that they are the victims of Arthur C. Clarke's Third Law, which states that 'Any sufficiently advanced technology is indistinguishable from magic.' For 'magic' read religion.

We may wonder at the naïvety of such unsophisticated people, but imagine travelling back in time and finding yourself in a primitive society long before the Abrahamic religions had been established. The people you meet are deeply religious: they worship the sun. Without the sun to ripen their crops they will starve, so every spring they sacrifice a young virgin to propitiate the sun god and beseech him to bless them with his powerful rays. And it works every time. Some years the clouds cover the sun for too long during the crucial ripening process, but the priests always have an explanation for that, usually connected to a lack of devotion by the people and inadequate offerings to the sun god.

You tell them you find this rite barbarous, and point out that the sun will shine whether they make their sacrifice or not. They tell you they'd rather not take that chance, thanks all the same, and ask what gods you believe in. You say you are a Christian and there is only one God and he created everything – including the sun and all the other stars. Then you set about explaining Christianity: God sent an angel to earth to impregnate a virgin and when the baby was born he was really the son of God, even though he was born to a virgin. You point out that, unlike theirs, yours is a God of love. In fact, the Christian God loves everyone so much that he arranged to have his own son brutally killed because that would somehow atone for all our sins. But being killed was a good thing because after he died he rose from the dead and ascended into heaven.

They find this a little puzzling and ask how you worship this God. You say something about eating his body and drinking his blood. They appear to find this pretty barbaric but you explain it's not *really* his body and blood because the rules about that were changed quite a long time ago. And it's not really just one God, or even two. It's three because there's the Holy Spirit as well. It's a trinity. Three in one. They look even more puzzled.

The ancients might also ask what sort of sacrifices you make to your god. For a horrible moment you are tempted by this idea. The image of certain politicians or reality-television 'celebrities' being disembowelled on the altar at St Saviour's flashes through your mind. But then you imagine what the fierce lady who runs the Mothers' Union would say about having to clean up the mess afterwards. Instead you say that your God is not vengeful and does not seek sacrifices. But if you are honest you will also say that your fellow Christians have killed vast numbers of people in the name of your religion over the centuries and your Holy Book speaks with approval of those who commit mass murder – children included – in the name of the Lord. Might they not find this a tad strange too – perhaps just as odd as we find their religion?

They might ask you what happens to those in your society who refuse to worship your god. Naturally, they put their blasphemers to death. You will say that in your country blasphemers may be ticked off by the high priests, who will do a great deal of tut-tutting, but no one else will take much notice. You might also point out that other religions take that sort of thing rather more seriously. If you upset certain extremist Muslims you may find yourself gunned down in the street or blown to bits by a suicide bomber who may believe he is going to paradise where his needs will be catered for by dozens of virgins. By now your listeners will be looking even more puzzled. They might even be wondering who are the primitives and who the civilised.

But whatever divides the followers of different religious faiths, two things unite them. One is that they believe theirs is the only true religion. The other is that they cannot prove it. Which doesn't stop them trying – often with bizarre results.

Every so often someone will find the 'bones of Jesus' or discover that he had a brother or a son who played in defence for Bethlehem United. Old Testament enthusiasts occasionally discover the Garden of Eden. I confidently expect the next 'discovery' to prove that it still exists in some remote corner of the globe and turns out to be a very nice place indeed – including a lovely lake where Noah keeps his ark and takes Adam and Eve for rides when they get bored with eating apples and being tempted by serpents. The most popular tourist attraction is the burning bush and the tasteful display featuring the tablets of stone bearing the Ten Commandments. Get there at the right time and Moses himself will give you a guided tour, explain how it all happened and sell you a charming replica of the tablets complete with imitation leather carrying case. You might even pick up a small piece of the True Cross – which must have been a very big cross indeed, given how many pieces exist as holy relics throughout Christendom.

There is a serious point to the parody. Dan Brown, with *The Da Vinci Code*, may have made more money out of it than anyone else in literary history, but plenty of others have done very well from persuading a gullible public that they have unearthed some world-changing truth about the existence or non-existence of God. I say 'gullible', but that's not fair. A better word might be 'vulnerable'.

Some people are fortunate enough to have an unshakeable belief. It is the foundation upon which everything in their lives can sit securely. Most of us are not so lucky or (if you prefer) so blessed. Many of us worry away at it, just as I did when I was a little boy on that disused aerodrome in Cardiff nearly sixty years ago, trying to find answers that might explain the great mystery. And some are so desperate that they will clutch at almost anything if it seems to support what they want to believe, even though every one of their instincts should tell them it's nonsense. They insist that the image that appears in the bowl of custard when you sprinkle nutmeg on it is the face of Jesus. Or that the fragment of tatty old cloth you buy from the excitable man in the Moroccan market is a piece of the Turin Shroud in which Jesus's body was buried – even though the 'genuine' shroud turned out to be a medieval fake.

There may be a dozen chemical explanations for why a particular statue of the Virgin has moisture seeping from its eyes, but it's enormously comforting to some people to believe that Mary is sending them a profound message by weeping. And the same goes for the stigmata that miraculously appear on the old priest in some sleepy Italian village every Good Friday morning. As I write this I'm looking at a picture in the *Daily Mail* of a scan of a baby in the late stages of gestation. The mother is convinced (and so are her friends and relatives) that her unborn baby has the face of Jesus. I wonder how they recognised him without the beard.

*   *   *

Sometimes the revelations come wrapped in apparently respectable covers. We had one in March 2006 from no less a figure than James Cameron, the Hollywood director who gave us *Titanic*, a film long on stunning special effects and short on pretty much everything else. I still marvel at the way two third-class passengers, young lovers, were able to stand with arms spread wide, hair ruffled by the breeze, on the prow of the great ship with no officer telling them that if they didn't stop behaving so stupidly and dangerously they'd be locked in the brig. Perhaps it helped that they were Leonard DiCaprio and Kate Winslet. It was an ambitious film – but nothing like as ambitious as Mr Cameron's Jesus epic.

This came in the form of a documentary, *The Lost Tomb of Jesus*, which 'revealed' that two ossuaries dug up in Jerusalem in 1980 had once held the body of Jesus. So impressed was Mr Cameron with this world-shattering discovery that he had the ossuaries – cream-coloured limestone coffins – flown to New York to be displayed at a news conference publicising his film. Mr Cameron, who has never been a man for modest understatement, told his audience, 'It doesn't get bigger than this.'

He was right in one sense. If the coffin had once contained the bones of Jesus, Christianity is built on a lie or, at the very least, a false foundation. You do not need to be a professor of divinity or the Archbishop of Canterbury to know that if Jesus did not rise from the dead and ascend, body and soul, into heaven, he was no more than a mere mortal. He might have been a good man who inspired his followers to establish a great church, but that's all he was. He was not the son of God. Even St Paul acknowledged two thousand years ago that 'if Christ is not raised . . . then our faith is in vain'. And by 'raised' he meant that the body of Jesus was physically raised to heaven. You either believe that or you do not. Mr Cameron made another claim. He had 'evidence' that Jesus had married Mary Magdalene and fathered a son they called Judah. The bones of Judah were, it seems, in another coffin.

So, that's the core of the New Testament story blown away. Jesus did not arise from the tomb after three days and he did not ascend physically into heaven. He died here on Earth – not once but twice – and was buried here on Earth. As it happens, Dan Brown wrote something similar to the 'Jesus and Mary' tale in *The Da Vinci Code*, but at least he had the good grace to publish it as fiction.

But what of Cameron's 'evidence'? The Israeli Antiquities Authority confirmed that the ossuaries were inscribed with the names of Jesus and Mary. Not only that, but Jesus was described as 'son of Joseph' and Mary 'daughter of Matthew'. All of which sounds impressive until you ask scholars how common those names happened to be in Biblical times. The answer is, very. Indeed, Dr Bruce Longenecker, a New Testament expert at St Andrews University, reckons that the Aramaic versions of Jesus, Mary, Joseph and Matthew accounted for nearly forty per cent of all names in that area of the Middle East at that time, which reduces the odds on a coincidence a bit.

But there's something else about these world-shattering discoveries. On closer inspection you often find that someone else has been there before you. I vaguely recalled the 'Jesus bones' stories from some other documentary I'd seen about ten years ago so I checked up. For once my memory served me well.

The reporter for the BBC programme had been the redoubtable and reliable Joan Bakewell. She described being taken, in 1996, to a dusty ware-house in the suburbs of Jerusalem where they had uncovered six ossuaries. Back in 1980 (the date ring a bell?) explosives being used in the building of new apartments in south Jerusalem had blasted open a tomb from the first century AD. In the tomb were the ossuaries. And inscribed on them were the names of Jesus, Mary, Joseph, Matthew and (more bells ringing?) Judah 'son of Jesus'. So far, so similar, but the difference between the Bakewell programme and the Cameron documentary lay in approach. Here's how Bakewell described what she had concluded:

> So much is fact. Neither then nor at any point later did we make any specific religious claims for these ossuaries. We merely asked the question: 'What if . . . the body of Jesus were to be discovered?' It was an idea appropriate for Easter Sunday. We called the programme *The Body in Question*.

So, in the hands of Bakewell and her team, the discovery of the ossuaries produces an idea 'appropriate for Easter Sunday'. In the hands of a famous Hollywood director, it becomes the biggest (or perhaps even he would admit the *second* biggest) story ever told. But what's interesting is the reaction to the two films.

When Bakewell's was broadcast, she said, 'All hell broke loose.' The *Daily Telegraph* said the programme was 'one of the silliest questionings' of the truth of the resurrection. It was 'ridiculed and denounced' across the press. The BBC's religious department 'came under pressure from within and without and had to make mumbling sounds of regret'. Bakewell also recalls how Keith Ward, then Regius Professor of Divinity at Oxford, declared, 'If it [the body] were found and validated in some way, I would cease to be a Christian.'

When Cameron's programme was broadcast pretty well every newspaper reported his claims, often on the front page. But mostly it was done in the way that you would report the antics of a well-known character who was embarrassingly prone to showing off. It's true that he had DNA tests carried out, something that was not available to Joan Bakewell, but he made claims for the results that could not be justified. He said the DNA tests proved that 'Jesus' and 'Mary' were not maternally related, so they must have been a couple. Hogwash. You can certainly speculate that – even assuming they were the 'real' Jesus and Mary – they may have had some other family relationship. They could, for instance, have been cousins. You cannot claim, as he did, that it proves they were a couple. Almost nobody, I think it's fair to say, took him or his programme seriously. And yet it became a big story.

*   *   *

So what is the truth in all this? God knows. Or not, as the case may be. And that isn't meant to be facetious. If there can be no proof that Jesus was born of a virgin, rose again after his death on the cross and ascended bodily into heaven, then it follows that it is a matter of belief. Believers say there is evidence – and it is to be found in the Gospels. The more knowledgeable will quote the Gospels endlessly to 'prove' their point and back up their quotes with, literally, chapter and verse. But there are two problems with all this.

One is the dubious nature of the evidence: the inconsistencies and the contradictions between the different accounts. And the other is that the Bible is convincing only if you approach it prepared to believe that it is divinely inspired, which is difficult if you don't believe in God. Those who are sceptical are more likely to see the contradictions than the 'proof'.

Obviously you would expect contradictions in such a collection of ancient writings. The New Testament accounts of the life and resurrection of Jesus were written about a generation after his death and inevitably relied on memory and anecdote rather than first-hand eyewitness testimony. Paul, who wrote the oldest parts of the New Testament and is regarded as the most influential of its writers, never met Jesus and has little to say about the historical facts of his life. The point about the Gospels is that they were the work of a group of men who had a particular message to impart and a mission to accomplish: that Jesus was the risen Lord. It may be that they were doing their best to provide an accurate story of his life. And, remember, they were also trying to build a church.

They had to have a dramatic story to capture the imagination and, ideally, the hearts and minds of those who heard their story. Something we shall never know is the extent to which that overriding ambition influenced their stories, but since they were mere mortals we can assume they were not immune to a touch of exaggeration in their own cause. What is beyond doubt is that they succeeded in the most spectacular way. The Christian faith has endured for two thousand years and has attracted billions of worshippers over the millennia.

Islam has been spectacularly successful too. In the seventh century Muhammad – believed by Muslims to be the last prophet in a line that includes Abraham, Moses and Jesus – founded his strict monotheistic religion in the Arab world. Until then Arabs worshipped many different gods and there was a great deal of lawlessness. Within a century Islam had conquered an area greater than the Roman Empire at its height. Today it is the sole religion of almost every Arab country and many in Africa.

The oldest of the great monotheistic religions is Judaism. It is reckoned by scholars to be 3,800 years since Abraham made the covenant with God in the name of the children of Israel.

And how long has God been around? For ever. Obviously. If you buy into any of the three Abrahamic religions you buy into the notion that God created the world and everything in it. But how many of us believe that?

PART THREE

State of the Nation

7

Britain has become a godless nation – or so we are often told. It is easy to believe it if you wander into a typical parish church on a Sunday morning. Finding a space on the pews is even less difficult than finding a weed in the overgrown churchyard – putting aside Easter and Christmas. Church attendance has been falling steadily since the 1950s. For the vast majority of the population Sunday is a day for shopping rather than worship. In the suburbs and the shires it is the tills that ring out to summon the faithful rather than the bells.

God may not be 'dead', as the German philosopher Nietzsche is quoted as saying, but you might gain the impression that his established church in Britain is on a life-support machine. Perhaps we have lost our fear that if we don't go to church we won't go to heaven. Or maybe we side with Machiavelli, who claimed that he'd prefer to go to hell because the company would be much more interesting. In hell you would be with the 'popes, kings and princes, while in heaven there are only beggars, monks, hermits and apostles'.

Yet look past the parish church on a Sunday morning, with its air of genteel shabbiness and the inevitable appeal for money to mend the roof, and a different picture begins to emerge. The building in the next street that was once a church may now be a mosque and on Fridays it will probably be full. Islam is thriving in Britain. In 2006 the most popular boys' name was Jack but the second was Muhammad. Some studies show that Islam is the fastest growing religion in Europe and is likely to grow even faster: the birth-rate among Muslims may be three times as high in some European countries as it is among non-Muslims. If the present trend continues, it has been calculated, France will be a predominantly Muslim country in a generation or so.

The evangelical wing of the Anglican Church has done well too. As I mentioned earlier, the charismatics and the happy-clappies have a lot to clap about in terms of bums on pews. The 'Alpha Courses' seem to have been designed with young, middle-class professionals in mind. Whether that's the case or not, they have been phenomenally successful. By the end of 2006 it was being claimed that more than eight million people had signed up for them.

Still, we have a long way to go before we catch up with the United States. A few years ago the humanist writer Michael Shermer said that never in history have so many Americans believed in God. Mr Shermer is the director of the Skeptics Society and publisher of *Skeptic* magazine and the figures prove him right. In no other country in the developed world does such a large proportion of the population believe. A frighteningly large number – one Gallup poll suggested more than half – are creationists. Other polls suggest that about forty per cent believe Jesus will return to judge the living and the dead some time in the next fifty years.

Something similar has been happening on other continents. The Chief Rabbi, Sir Jonathan Sacks, wrote in 2002 about a 'revival of evangelical Protestantism' sweeping across Latin America, sub-Saharan Africa, the Philippines, South Korea and even (in spite of persecution) China.

Prospect, a magazine that has an influence out of proportion to its tiny circulation and a reputation for its rigorously highbrow approach, had this headline on its front cover at the end of 2006:

God Returns to Europe

Eric Kaufmann of Birkbeck College, who wrote the piece, said there is a religious revival 'that may be as profound as that which changed the course of the Roman empire in the fourth century'. He based his conclusions on demographic research. Dr Kaufmann analysed data from ten western European countries from the period 1981–2004 and found, unsurprisingly, that most babies are born to women who are married and fairly young. But he also found that if a woman is religious she is likely to have more children than if she is not. You would expect that to be the case in Catholic countries, such as Italy and Ireland, where birth control is less likely to be practised but it applies to Protestant countries, such as Holland and Britain, too. As Dr Kaufmann put it, western Europe 'has long been seen as leading the world in secular modernisation, but now that trend appears to be losing its force'.

An academic's research is more reliable than the reaction to a Radio 4 series, but even so it was hard to ignore the size of the response from the audience to *Humphrys in Search of God*.

But obviously it is foolish to make judgements on the basis of a self-selecting sample. The number of people who write may reflect the depth of feeling rather than the breadth, and there is no way of telling how large a section of the population they represent. Those empty pews may be a more accurate reflection than the bulging postbags, so I decided to approach things a bit more scientifically. I asked the internet polling organisation YouGov to carry out a survey in Britain. I wanted to find out not just how many of us believe in God but what we mean when we talk about belief.

At one end of the spectrum are Jews, Christians and Muslims who (mostly) have a pretty clear idea of what they mean. They are theists. They believe in one God who created everything and still gets involved in the world. He knows about every sparrow that falls.

At the other end are atheists. They do not believe in a 'supernatural' god. Full stop.

Somewhere in the middle are deists, who believe God created everything and then said in effect, 'That's it. I've done my bit. Now let 'em get on with it.'

And then there are those who believe (if that's the right word) in nature. They acknowledge a powerful force at work in the world but are more likely to sense it in a great oak tree than in the idea of a supernatural god. They may be spiritual or even mystical, but they are not religious. They are usually called pantheists. Within these categories there are endless variations.

That's one of the reasons why it is pointless to ask: 'Do you believe in God?' The only sensible answer must be: 'Depends what you mean by God.' So, for the purpose of the YouGov survey, I framed the first question in more specific terms. Here's the result – with all the figures representing a percentage of the 2,200 people who took part.

Which of these comes closest to your belief?

- I believe in a personal God who created the world and hears my prayers   22
- I believe God created everything but then left us to get on with it.   6
- I believe in 'something' but I'm not sure what   26
- I would like to believe and I envy those who do but cannot believe for myself   5
- I am an agnostic. I don't think it is possible to know if there is a God or not.   9
- I am an atheist. The whole notion of a supernatural God is nonsense.   16
- I'm really not sure what I believe and I don't give it much thought   10

- Other   3
- Don't know   3

This may not prove Eric Kaufmann's contention that we are undergoing an extraordinary religious revival, but it does prove that the militant atheists have a tough fight on their hands. Fewer than one in six think of themselves as atheists. It's an interesting reflection on the kind of society we have become. We spend more, borrow more and save less than we have ever done. One survey after another shows that we are more materialistic than we have ever been. And yet most of us either believe, or want to believe, in something beyond the material. So how do we demonstrate our spirituality? My next question was about prayer.

How often do you pray?

- I pray every night   10
- I pray fairly regularly   14
- I hardly ever pray   31
- I do not pray at all   43
- Don't know   2

These answers need to be looked at in the light of the first set of responses. More than half of those who say they believe in a personal God cannot be bothered to pray to him every night.

This strikes me as rather bizarre. If you really believed that God hears your prayers, wouldn't you be getting down on your knees every night? It could be that there are millions who don't have anything to pray for on a daily basis, but that seems unlikely. Even if your own life is utterly perfect in every respect, might you not want to offer up a prayer for those who are a little less fortunate – or maybe just to commune with God? Or perhaps we prefer to pray in public. Let's see.

How often do you attend a place of worship?

- More than once a week   2
- Once a week   4
- Two or three times a month   3
- Once a month   2
- Less than once a month   8
- Only for special occasions such as weddings and funerals   62
- Never   18
- Don't know   1

So, not only are the faithful failing to pray every night, they're not bothering to go to their place of worship either. Even if we include those who go only once a month the number of worshippers barely tops one in ten. That's fewer than half of those who say they believe in a personal God, and that's a bit odd too, isn't it? On the face of it, it seems to support some earlier surveys that suggest organised religion is in a state of near terminal decline. A study for the University of Manchester based on 1990s data found that the proportion of people who believe in God was dropping faster than the proportion who attend a place of worship and parents had only a 50–50 chance of passing on belief to their offspring.

The Church of England's own regular surveys suggest that what they call 'usual Sunday attendance', is still falling. But that's not the whole picture, as my own results show. Applied to the whole adult population, the YouGov findings suggest that about four million people attend a place of worship every month, and the figures are much higher in areas where the population is more ethnically diverse. Some of the most successful churches in Britain are those with largely black congregations. Many Roman Catholic churches are having to turn away the faithful at the door – mainly because of the large numbers of people coming to Britain from Poland. At this rate, the Catholic Church will be bigger here than the Church of England in a few years.

The YouGov survey reveals something else

about our attitude to religion that I found intriguing and, if I were a church leader, it would worry me. I wanted to know how big an influence religion is seen to have on this country. More than half said it was either very significant or fairly significant – which might be considered encouraging to believers. But that led to my next question, which dealt with whether people think it a beneficial or harmful influence. And a remarkable 42 per cent thought it was harmful.

Obviously one explanation for this might be the publicity attracted by a handful of mad mullahs and their hate-filled rhetoric. The Roman Catholic Archbishop of Birmingham, Vincent Nichols, thinks the general unease in the West over Islam gives other religions a bad name. In 2007 he said:

> The acts of terrorism have shaken up people's perception of the presence of faiths in this country and around the world, and I just wish there was a bit more differentiation in the reflection about the role of faiths in society.

The response to the YouGov questions seems to support the Archbishop. Even though the dominant faith – by a massive margin – is Christianity, only 17 per cent thought the influence of religion was beneficial. That is even fewer than those who claim to believe in a personal God. And yet when we asked which of the main religions was 'most effective in getting its message across' only ten per cent said Islam, while 32 per cent said Christianity. As the Americans might put it, go figure.

So what are we to make of the survey's findings? Well, the first and most obvious conclusion is that a relatively small minority of us consider ourselves Christians in any meaningful sense. When we are asked to fill in our religion on official forms we might automatically write 'C of E' but most of us don't really mean it. It's just something to put in the box to satisfy the bureaucrats. The Anglican Church is struggling to hold on to its place as the spiritual home of the nation. And even if we do consider ourselves active believers with a faith in a personal God most of us cannot be bothered to go to church or even to spend a few minutes praying. What a strange way to demonstrate our faith. It's as if we are saying, 'Yes, I believe in God but that doesn't mean I have to do anything about it.' And yet very few of us are atheists. Overwhelmingly we want some sort of spiritual dimension to our lives.

The other conclusion must be that there is a growing suspicion of organised religion and the influence it is having on society. What many of us seem to be saying is that we may well be prepared to believe in God, but it will be a God of our own choosing and not necessarily the God of any ancient religion. I suspect one reason for this is our changing attitude to authority.

8

Let me try to draw a connection – it's pretty tenuous, I admit – between the great thinkers of the European Enlightenment and my own father. He was intelligent and had an enquiring mind but was almost totally uneducated. He had to leave school at thirteen because he'd lost his eyesight as a result of a bad attack of measles. He never read a book on philosophy or religion in his life. What he shared with the great figures of the Enlightenment was a deep distrust of the church establishment, the power it wielded over the lives of ordinary men and women, a belief in reason rather than dogma, and a refusal to be told what to think and what to believe.

At the heart of the Enlightenment was a rejection of the idea that religion – specifically the Christian Church – provided all the answers to everything we would ever need to know and could be relied on totally to tell us how to lead our lives. To believe otherwise was blasphemous. The

Enlightenment thinkers preferred science and rational enquiry to religious dogma and proscription. The more extreme wanted to do away with religion altogether. Those who were agnostic rather than atheist – and even some believers – challenged the intolerance of the Church and the grip in which it held the vast majority of the population through a combination of fear and superstition. They wanted to liberate people from the clutches of the clergy and free them to think their own thoughts instead of being forced to swallow the dogma that the clergy forced down their throats.

For obvious reasons, my father never articulated it in quite those terms, but he viewed the institutions of power with profound suspicion – all of them. He was once ordered to leave his local Conservative club because there was only one place left to sit and that happened to be beneath a portrait of the Queen. Rather than drink his beer beneath such a symbol, he went without his pint. Now *that*'s principle for you. Perhaps it seems odd that he was a Conservative, but that was because he was self-employed. He didn't like bosses any more than he liked monarchs and had been sacked for punching the foreman's nose just after he'd completed his apprenticeship as a french-polisher. The Tories were the lesser of two evils. He hated socialism.

As for the Church, he was happy to tolerate my mother's piety and affection for it so long as it made no demands of him. He might even, as far as I could tell, have believed in some sort of God. He never said and I never asked. In those days it wasn't the sort of thing working-class families like ours discussed. But he had an abiding distrust and dislike of the clergy – mostly, I think, because they thought they were a cut above ordinary people like him.

That can probably be traced to an experience he had as a young man when he was staying with his aunt at her little cottage in a Somerset village not long after the First World War had ended. They were about to sit down for Sunday lunch when the door burst open and the vicar strode in. Without so much as a by-your-leave, a tap on the door or even 'Good morning', he demanded to know why my great-aunt had not been at the morning service. She did a little bob – not quite a curtsy, but not far from it – and stammered some sort of apology. She tried to explain that she seldom had visitors and she'd been busy preparing lunch for her nephew whom she hadn't seen for a year and who had come from a long way away (the other side of the Severn estuary) but she'd make sure to turn up for evensong. He was having none of it. He barked at her, 'See that you do! Don't let it happen again!' and marched out without another word. He did not even acknowledge the presence of her guest.

My father was outraged and remembered that encounter in minute detail until his dying day. How *dare* the vicar treat his aunt with such disdain – exactly like a lord of the manor dealing with a serf! But those were the days of deference, especially in a rural backwater like Wellow in Somerset, when the working class knew its place and would never have dared to stand up to the authority of the vicar.

Deference began to die as the victorious but disillusioned soldiers returned from the war to a land that turned out not to be fit for heroes. They had been grievously let down by men who were supposed to be their betters and they were not about to forgive them for it – or to forget. The old deference has long been in the process of receiving the last rites. If it is not dead and buried by now, it is certainly gasping its last breath. We question and challenge all forms of authority, whether it be represented by the police or the head teacher, po-liticians, the monarchy or the Church. Especially, perhaps, the Church. Yet we were still looking to it for our moral guidelines until very recently.

*   *   *

Callum Brown, Professor of Religious and Cultural History at Dundee University, says we accepted a strict Christian moral code drawn from the teachings of evangelicals right up until the late 1950s. Christianity formed the identity of individual men and women of all classes. Today, he says, a vast chasm separates us from that world – the last high point when religion mattered deeply in British society and from which we drew that sense of identity. The culture of Christianity, he says,

> has gone in the Britain of the new millennium. Britain is showing the world how religion as we have known it can die.

In his book *The Death of Christian Britain*, Brown draws on what happened in the 1960s to reach his conclusion. A lot of nonsense has been written about that period. The idea that young men like me drifted around on a cloud of marijuana smoke, making love to any winsome young mini-skirted beauty who happened to catch our eye for more than a few moments, is very wide of the mark – as is the idea that all those lovely young women joined in enthusiastically. More's the pity. That may have been the case for a few daring and reckless young students, rock singers and their hangers-on in London, but if a working-class lad wanted to get high in Cardiff (or, I suspect, any other provincial town) he was more likely to do it with several pints of best bitter than with a badly rolled spliff. Yet something significant was going on and, according to Professor Brown, it was profoundly important for the Christian churches.

When women started burning their bras and demanding equality with men, they were repudiating the categorisation of their social identity that had been prevalent since the nineteenth century. For a hundred and fifty years or more, women had been expected to behave in a certain way. Apart from all the obvious requirements of them – mother, home-maker, loyal supporter to the wage-earning husband, provider of sex – their role was to be pious. They were to be the guardians of Christian culture, tradition and morality and to hand it on to the next generation. That's certainly how my mother saw her role. What Brown's work suggests is that the radicalisation of women in the 1960s broke that link. He writes about the simultaneous 'de-feminization of piety and the de-pietization of femininity'.

At that time we were also beginning to see the effect of enormous changes to the education system made a couple of decades earlier. Until the 1944 Education Act the Church of England ran a vast number of schools. The new law established free secondary education and most of the church schools were handed over to the state. Twenty years later, the man who was education secretary at the time, R. A. Butler, lamented what had happened to Christian teaching in the new state schools. It had reached such a point, he said, as to 'imperil the basis of the Christian character of the nation'. A slight exaggeration, perhaps, but let's not forget the provocative boast of the Jesuits: 'Give me the child until he is seven and I will give you the man.'

For all the cosmetic changes to the Christian Church over the decades, its essential nature is unchanged. If you had tried hugging your neighbour in my old church when I was a boy you'd probably have got a clout with a stout handbag. The vicar might swap his vestments for jeans after the service – or even, if it's an Anglican vicar, a mini-skirt – but the congregation still bows its head to the altar, if not literally in every church at least metaphorically.

The Church is, by its very nature, authoritarian. God is the boss and that's that. You do what he tells you if you want to win his approval and a place in heaven. You either acknowledge that or you don't. You may try desperately to find reasons for God's actions, but once you have accepted that he is the supreme being and the Church is the embodiment of his authority, you cannot question his right to demand your absolute obedience. You cannot cut a deal with God.

PART FOUR
The Interviews

9

The point of *Humphrys in Search of God* was not to question his authority. You would have to believe God existed to do that and obviously I approached it as a doubter. Nor was it to prove that God did or did not exist. That's an impossible task for reasons we have already discussed. For the purpose of the interviews, I wanted to know why, if God *does* exist, he behaves as he does.

Before I get on to the content of the interviews, let me offer a few thoughts on the process. People like me who spend most of our professional lives talking to other people on the radio or television have limited ambitions. The minimum is that we don't dry up on air and/or make a complete fool of ourselves.

I have done both over the years. I've dried up twice (I was very young at the time) and I have made a fool of myself more often than I am prepared to acknowledge. I was once so severely hung-over that I was not only incapable of asking any more questions of the politician to whom I was talking but I realised I had forgotten his name. That was also quite a long time ago and I learned my lesson: no more boozy nights before a programme.

What we really hope to achieve, though it doesn't happen often, is the interview that changes things. It is plastered across the newspapers the following morning and, in the cliché beloved by *Today*, 'sets the agenda'. When it does happen it is usually an accident of timing. You're just the lucky soul who gets the interview. A few months after he'd become prime minister, and was embroiled in his first scandal, Tony Blair told me that people thought he was 'a pretty straight kind of guy'. It was a memorable quote that would return to haunt him throughout his ten years in power, but he could have said it to anyone. It just happened to be me. Mostly it is unwise to expect a great deal from any one interview.

I thought my three "God" interviews would be different in one important sense. It's true that the potential for making a fool of myself was high. There was the title for a start – a real hostage to fortune. I knew I'd get a bit of stick and I did. The wittiest review was written by the Conservative MP Michael Gove in *The Times*. He created a fictional radio series entitled *God in Search of Humphrys*.

The big difference between this series and the *Today* programme was that they were meant to be personal conversations rather than news-breaking confrontations. I was effectively inviting leading figures in three of the world's great religions to convert me live on air. My poor interviewees must have felt a bit like the aspiring comedian in the office of a stony-faced showbiz agent when he's told, 'Go on then, make me laugh.'

As it happens, the Chief Rabbi saw the funny side. The first time I talked to him about appearing on the programme he asked me what I hoped to get out of the interview. 'It's simple enough,' I said. 'All you've got to do is convert me . . . turn me into a religious Jew.'

He put his hand on my arm, smiled rather sadly, and said, 'John, I wouldn't dream of it. You've got enough problems already.'

I'm not entirely sure he was joking. But neither was I. Not entirely. I do not want to be converted to Judaism any more than I want to become a Muslim or even to reclaim my Christian belief, but in many ways I would rather like to believe whole-heartedly in God. And, yes, I know how pathetic that will sound to many people reading this. When

I suggested the series to the controller of Radio 4, Mark Damazer, I half hoped he would turn it down, but maybe he fancied the idea of grumpy old Humphrys falling to his knees live on air, offering hosannas to his new saviour, promising to mend his ways and stop being beastly to politicians. It might have been good box office but no one would have believed it.

If you present a programme like *Today* you can expect criticism. I am either a Marxist or a Fascist. I'm in love with Labour or in thrall to the Tories. I'm too aggressive or too supine. I interrupt too much or I let them get away with endless waffle. I'm too cynical or too naïve.

I sometimes try to defend myself by pointing out that to be attacked by both sides simultaneously must mean I've got it about right but, of course, it means nothing of the sort. If the listener is offended by the way I conducted the interview, then as far as that listener is concerned I got it wrong.

Sometimes we accept the listeners' judgement and promise to do better next time. Mostly we don't. A presenter steeped in humility is as rare as a vegetarian tiger. Hubris, yes; humility, no. We defend ourselves to the last breath. But there is one rule we should never breach: we should not defend ourselves by attacking the interviewee. If I am asked in public what I think of a politician's performance, I keep my mouth shut. It's for the listener to make the judgement, not me. But I don't think that rule applies to something as personal as these three interviews, which is why I have indulged in some of what the Americans call 'Monday-morning quarter-backing' in these next chapters.

Many listeners have told me that if I have failed to 'find' God the fault must lie with me: I have not properly opened my heart. I have – like a broken-nosed doorman at a trendy nightclub – refused to allow him admission. Well, maybe. But maybe it's because my interviewees failed to make a decent case. Perhaps – as other listeners suggested – they were too hesitant: they should have grabbed me by the throat and bellowed into my ear until I gave in and accepted God as my saviour. Or something like that.

They were especially critical of the Archbishop of Canterbury, Rowan Williams. They said he himself seemed to be so full of doubt that he'd have had trouble persuading a two-year-old to eat his ice-cream. They wanted a lot less agonising and a lot more proclaiming his faith. I can see why a devout Christian might take that view, but I think it's mistaken. On the question of suffering I'd have been surprised if he'd had any pat answers – and he did not.

10

For those of us who started out as Christians, flirted with atheism and ended up as doubters, the question of a merciful God is a pretty big one. Indeed, for many people it is the killer question. At one stage it was for me. It's simple enough. We are told that God is merciful. We are told that God created everything. We are told that the only way to salvation is through belief in this merciful God. We are told that faith and goodness and virtue are always rewarded and that wickedness will be punished. Then we look around us and what do we see? Precisely the opposite.

We see appalling suffering and we see that it is usually the innocent — by which I mean those who have done least to deserve it — who suffer most.

- When forty tonnes of lethal gas were released in a terrible industrial accident in India the rich shareholders in the American company that allowed it to happen had to pay compensation to the survivors. They paid with dollars. The poor who worked in the factory and lived nearby paid with their lives. Twenty thousand people died as a result of the Bhopal accident in 1984. The company prospers to this day.

- When a cruise missile or a bomb hits the 'wrong' target the officer in charge may or may not face an inquiry. The people underneath the bomb lose their homes, their loved ones or their lives.

- When the crops fail in a poor country it may well be because the rain did not fall. But when people starve as a result it is usually because their corrupt leaders have stolen the aid that might have kept them alive. They end up with villas and private jets. The poor watch their children die.

The history of the past century tells us that tyrants tend to die in their beds – usually of old age. Of the three greatest mass murderers it was only Hitler who paid the price for his evil, with his cowardly exit. Mao and Stalin died with the praise of sycophants still sounding in their ears. Hitler's fatal mistake was to be too ambitious. Had he limited his wickedness to his own country he'd probably have got away with it. So, let's put an end to this nonsense of virtue being its own reward. It's not. Neither is God merciful. He's not. Not on this earth anyway.

The question of how and why a loving God could have created such a brutal world is hardly original. Theologians have worried away at it for centuries. Clever people like Roy Hattersley dismiss it out of hand. He says it is many years since he has wasted his time 'discussing the possibility that God, if he or she exists, might not be the bountiful deity that sentimental Christians claim'. Moreover, Lord Hattersley says he has

> . . . long passed the stage of intellectual naïvety that asks plaintive questions about how a God of love can allow so much suffering in the world that he has created.

All I can say to him is that if he's right there are an awful lot of intellectually naïve people out there. What strikes me as important is whether it is possible to reconcile a personal God who is supposed to listen to our prayers and take heed of them with a God who proceeds to ignore them. I'll come on to the question of prayer and free will later, but let's deal with suffering first. I spoke at some length to my three interviewees about it and I wanted to make it personal, rather than worry away at the finer theological niceties.

Nicky Gumbel, the barrister who was ordained in the Church of England and founded the Alpha Course, says Christianity is 'first and foremost about relationships' and is about

> a person more than a philosophy . . . It is about the most important relationship of all: our relationship with the God who made us.

That was why, when I raised the question of a merciful God with the Archbishop of Canterbury, I used the suffering of a child to make the point. He told me the child suffers 'because certain causes, certain processes have kicked in'. So the question is why God creates those 'processes' knowing – and he can hardly claim ignorance because he's meant to know everything, isn't he? – that they will cause intolerable suffering. How could he allow the suffering of, for instance, a mother watching her child dying of cancer? The Archbishop's first response was 'We don't quite know why.' Here's how the conversation went after that.

> RW: My faith tells me, and it's very hard to believe in these circumstances, but it tells me – and I trust this – that the world is such that suffering arises in these unspeakable ways. It also tells me that what God can do with those

circumstances and those persons is not exhausted by the world. There's more.

JH: Sorry . . . More what?

RW: God has more to give. God has more to do with the mother, the child, whatever the circumstances are. God has an eternity in which to heal or to lead forward the people involved in those circumstances. I don't mean make it up to them, but I mean that there's a future.

JH: But the child is dead. The parents' lives have been destroyed.

RW: Humanly speaking that's the end of the story and that's the nightmare. Faith says that's not the end of the story.

JH: Because we'll go to heaven?

RW: God has eternity in which to go on working with those persons.

JH: So the best you can offer to the person whose child has died from cancer, the best you can offer those parents, is 'Bear up . . . there's a reason . . . your reward will be in heaven'?

RW: No.

JH: Is that it?

RW: No, that's not what I want to offer at all, because the conversation I'd have in those circumstances isn't the kind of conversation I'd have here. For one thing . . . if someone says,

'Where's God in that situation?' it would have to be answered partly in terms of 'Where are the people who should be alongside those who are suffering, offering what love and healing they can?' Whether in the name of God or not, the act of God is there as well. I'm not saying there's a purpose in the sense that God has said, 'Oh, yes, for that goal, for that end I will devise this disaster, or even that there's a reward in heaven.' I'd say there's hope.

JH: Hope of what?

RW: Hope of healing.

JH: When?

RW: In God's perspective, in God's time, maybe within this world and maybe not. And part of the difficulty of living with faith is the knowledge which you've underlined so powerfully, that for some people in our time frame in this world there is not that kind of healing. It's not there. And that's not easy to face or to live with.

JH: But you can live with it?

RW: Just . . . just.

This struck me as an extraordinary moment in the interview. I recorded more than five hours of conversation for the series and that answer –

barely a couple of seconds – seemed to me the most telling. Rowan Williams is the leader of seventy million Anglicans, one of the most highly regarded theologians and scholars of his generation, a man of great spirituality, and there he was, sitting in front of me, admitting that he can only 'just' live with the belief that God is the God of mercy who heals the suffering. Just.

Muslims also believe in a merciful God. The Koran describes Muhammad as a Prophet of Mercy. Muslims begin all their acts, including worship, with the words: 'In the name of God, the compassionate, the merciful'. For the second of my interviews I spoke to the leading Muslim academic Professor Tariq Ramadan. Here's how he dealt with my questions about suffering.

> *TR*: We were born innocent (this is the difference between the Jewish, the Christian and the Muslim tradition) and we became responsible and we have to deal with our own responsibility. So we are responsible at a certain age. You know, all the kids, all the children are going to paradise, according to the Islamic tradition, because they are innocent.
>
> *JH*: So it's all right if they suffer on this earth in the knowledge that they will go to paradise?

TR: No . . . It's difficult to accept it as something which is intellectually understandable. But this is life, we are going to suffer because at the end of the day life is suffering.

JH: But why did God want that to happen?

TR: I don't know why sometimes he makes me happy or sad, but this is life. The only thing which I know is that we have responsibility trying to do our best with what we do and what we are facing. That's it. We have a verse in the Koran: 'He creates death and life in order to put you in a test.' It's to test you. This is a test. You are a test for me, because you are not me, you are different from me. So our encounter is full of happiness, potential happiness, and a possible threat, a possible sadness and possible difficulties, because diversity is a gift and a problem at the same time. Suffering is a gift and a problem . . . we live with this with great difficulty. And sometimes out of our suffering we become better, we become wiser, we become more knowledgeable about life.

JH: *We* might, you and I, but our *children*?

TR: Maybe not . . . When I'm travelling in southern countries and I see what I see, these children and these kids dying, it's very difficult. But I am not dealing with it in an exclusively rational way. Not everything is rational . . . not everything should be put in our logic . . . This is why humility means you don't know everything, you don't understand everything, but deal the best way you can with what you know, what you understand.

JH: So it is blind faith in the end.

TR: Sometimes people say you have double talk! I said exactly the opposite of what you heard. I said . . .

JH: You said you look at the suffering child and you do not know why that child is being allowed to suffer, but in the end you have to accept it. If that is not blind faith I don't know what is.

TR: No, it's not blind faith. I said something else which you didn't quote right. I said you have to do your best with what you know and what you can. This is exactly the opposite. It is not blind faith.

JH: Isn't it?

TR: We are dealing with people who are suffering. What you can do when you are a doctor, when you are a social worker, you do your best to make them suffer less. You are comparing what I am saying to passivity. It's exactly the opposite. And I refuse passivity and fatalism in order to say you have to do

> what you can do to change the morality of this world for the better. And in the end every human being is a reformer. You reform your own self, you reform your family, you reform your society, you reform around you. Whatever you can do, do it . . . But remain humble because, at the end, you cannot change everything and you have to accept the reality of life.

Islam is the youngest of the Abrahamic religions and Judaism is the oldest. In *The God Delusion* Richard Dawkins raids his thesaurus for adjectives to describe the God of the Old Testament:

> Arguably the most unpleasant character in all fiction; jealous and proud of it; a petty, unjust, unforgiving control-freak; a vindictive, bloodthirsty ethnic cleanser; a misogynistic, homophobic, racist, infanticidal, genocidal, filicidal, pestilential, megalomaniacal, sadomasochistic, capriciously malevolent bully.

All of which makes Gore Vidal's description of the Old Testament – a 'barbaric Bronze Age text' – look like a rave review.

The Chief Rabbi, Sir Jonathan Sacks, the last of my interviewees, unsurprisingly sees things rather differently:

Ours is the first God of mercy in the history of the human spirit and every book in the Bible is saturated with that.

So how do we square that with what people like Dawkins and Vidal find in the Bible? The answer is, of course, that they are all correct. It's easy to find the cruel, bloodthirsty God and it's easy to find the merciful God. It depends where you look. But surely you cannot ignore what God did to the founding father himself, to Abraham. He presented him with an impossible demand: if you believe in me you must sacrifice your child. Does that sound like a God of mercy?

JS: We know that child sacrifice was incredibly widespread in the ancient world. We know that from every kind of archaeological evidence. Child sacrifice, which is referred to many times in the Hebrew Bible as the most abominable of all acts, was the kind of thing you expected a god to ask of you. It's what gods regularly asked of their devotees. The essence of the story of Abraham is that at the critical moment God says, 'Stop – I am not that kind of god.'

JH: So he played with him. He was toying with him.

161

JS: He was teaching him. I think you must have had pretty hairy moments when you were first learning to drive, John, where your driving instructor slammed on the brakes and said, 'I did that just so you should learn exactly what would happen if you don't listen carefully.' So God slammed on the brakes. It was the most effective way of all of history.

JH: So it was a stunt, then?

JS: No, it was a learning experience, John, which is what we all need. And it was the revolutionary moment at which God says, 'I do not demand human sacrifices. I am not the God of the Greeks, of the Romans, of the Aztecs, I am the God that holds that life is holy. You must learn to cherish your children. And from the days of Abraham to today, John, Jews are the most child-centred of all civilisations. We live for our children.

But if God 'holds that life is holy' and we must learn to 'cherish our children', why does he allow so many children to suffer so terribly? How can anyone who has seen their own child suffer and die hold on to their faith?

JS: To my mind, faith lies in the question. If you didn't have faith you wouldn't ask the question.

If I did not believe in a just and law-abiding

God, I would not find injustice and human suffering worthy of question whatsoever. After all, the universe, if it has no God, is utterly indifferent to my existence. It's blind to my hopes and deaf to my prayers. So if I have no faith I can't ask the question. Faith is in the question. That question that you've just asked me is the question Abraham asked God and Moses and Jeremiah and Job. And the refusal to give an easy answer is in Judaism the essence of faith. God says, 'If you knew why this suffering happens you would live with it, you would accept it as the will of God. I don't want you to accept it as the will of God. I want you to go out there and heal the sick, feed the hungry, tend those who are injured. I want you to be', in that wonderful and very distinctive Jewish phrase, 'my partners in the work of creation.' So Judaism is in the question, not in the answer.

JH: I have to say that if a politician said to me, 'That's a most difficult question. If I give you the answer it will destroy your faith in the political system, in the democratic process, so it's very important that that question not be answered,' I'd think, he's having me on here.

JS: You would think a politician was trying to evade the issue . . .

JH: I would . . .

JS: . . . but if your teacher in school gave you the same answer . . .

JH: . . . I'd think the same . . .

JS: . . . you would understand that your teacher is challenging you by saying, 'I'm sorry, John, I can't answer you that, you would have to live with that.'

JH: The teacher would be *unable* to answer it. You are saying that that question is capable of being answered.

JS: It is perfectly capable of being answered.

JH: Well, answer it.

JS: But if we answered it we would not be what God wants us to be. Let me, if I can, explain. A parent of a baby who is ill, who is crying, gives that baby some medicine even though they know that baby's going to cry even more, because they know that suffering in the short term is justified in order to make the baby better in the long term. If we take the stance that suffering in the short term is necessary for good in the long term, we would accept suffering as God's will. God does not want us to accept suffering as his will. God wants us to fight suffering. Judaism is God's call to us to accept responsibility.

JH: For what?

JS: For creating a social order that does honour to the human person as God's image. That is the great challenge of creating the just and gracious society.

JH: But if God is omnipotent why did he not simply say, 'Here is this perfect structure that you can go off and inhabit and worship me'?

JS: John, you are a father. Why didn't you say to your child, 'Here it is, this is what life is. What you've got to do is go and do exactly what I've told you and you'll be happy and I'll be happy'? Because you know that your child is not going to grow into an adult unless you give that child the space to make mistakes and to learn by it.

JH: That's true, but you're missing out a crucial fact in the relationship between father and child and that is that we – and you're a father as well – will do anything, anything at all, to prevent our children suffering.

JS: Yeah, of course.

JH: I wouldn't say, 'Go off, try it, and it may end up with your painful death.'

JS: One hundred per cent.

JH: I wouldn't say that.

JS: Judaism, if I may explain something which is very hard for a western mind to grapple with, sees truth as set in time. A child aged five and a child aged twenty-five are not the same people. And so in the very early years of childhood a parent is much more protective of children than he is when they're twenty-five. And so we find in the Bible, at the very childhood of the Jewish people, God intervenes to rescue them. He rescues them from slavery, he takes them out of Egypt, he leads them across the Red Sea, he does miracles, he gives them water to drink and food to eat. He is a very protective father.

JH: And then he abandons them.

JS: No, he doesn't at all abandon them. God has not at all abandoned us to this day.

JH: He let the Holocaust happen.

JS: I am sometimes asked where was God in Auschwitz.

JH: And you answer, 'Where was man in Auschwitz?'

JS: And I answer as follows: 'God was in Auschwitz in the command 'thou shalt not murder'; in the words 'you shall not oppress the stranger'; in the words 'your brother's blood cries to me from the ground'. God was saying those things to the German people and they didn't listen. I cannot let human beings off the hook by blaming things on

God. If I do, then I'm betraying the mission that he sent me and sent all of us. We cannot escape from responsibility. Judaism is God's call to responsibility.

The contrast between the approaches of the Archbishop and the Chief Rabbi to the question of a merciful God is striking. Where Rowan Williams was hesitant, Jonathan Sacks was force-ful: 'If you didn't have faith you wouldn't ask the question . . . Faith is in the question.'

It's clever, isn't it? Merely to ask the question, he says, is proof of faith. I've no doubt Sacks is himself a man of great faith and he clearly believes what he says. The problem with his answer is that it shuts down the question. You can't take it anywhere. You can argue as passionately as you like that the question has been raised through the ages by doubters, but in the end you come up against the Sacks roadblock: they can't really be doubters because if they were they wouldn't be asking the question.

But why not? Of course he's right that atheists don't ask the question. They *know* there is no God so, by definition, the question does not arise for them. Fundamentalist believers don't ask either. They have the enviable ability to discard the tricky bits and accept only that which shores up their belief. They close off the argument, too, though in a less elegant way than the Chief Rabbi. They say, 'If God does it this way there must be a reason for it because God is God and he wouldn't do it unless it were the right thing to do.' And you can't argue with that, can you?

But doubters have that need because they do *not* know. They do not know that God exists and neither do they know that he doesn't exist. So they ask questions. Rowan Williams may talk about God having 'an eternity in which to heal' but we don't. We mere mortals have just one life. In fairness to the Archbishop, he's not a man for the glib answer. He resisted my temptation to say their 'reward will be in heaven'. The best that he could offer was that there is 'hope . . . hope of healing'.

Well, I'm afraid that won't do. I think Rowan Williams knows it won't do. So what can be said to those who suffer in this world at the hands of others? At the core of the believers' defence is free will.

11

For reasons I made clear earlier, I belong to the vast majority of the population who attend church only for special occasions such as weddings and funerals – and even then reluctantly. I made an exception a few years ago when I was invited by my local vicar to attend the Sunday-morning service and deliver the sermon. I told him I was flattered to be asked but pointed out the obvious drawback: I was not sure that I believed in God. He was completely unfazed. 'No problem,' he said. 'Lots of people don't, but that's no reason we shouldn't hear what they have to say.'

I confess that puzzled me a bit. I'd assumed that the whole point of going to church was to worship God, and the sermon was meant to reassure you that you were backing the right horse. I have heard many sermons in my time – most of them pretty dire – but can't recall the vicar telling us that we might as well be down the pub having a good time and God won't mind because he doesn't really exist. Which was more or less what I told the vicar I would be saying.

But times have changed and the Church of England has (mostly) changed with them, and my vicar wasn't going to let a small matter like my lack of faith get in the way. So I figured that if he wanted me to turn his place of worship into a debating society, who was I to resist? I delivered my sermon and went my way feeling only slightly foolish.

The next time I sat in the pews, a few years later, was for the funeral of my much-mourned colleague Nick Clarke. St Mary Abbots in Kensington was packed with the great and the good and, more importantly, with Nick's friends. The choir was superb and the eulogies perfectly judged. The problem was the vicar, Gillean Craig.

That may sound a little harsh. He is, I'm sure, a thoroughly godly man doing a good job of running his magnificent church. But in the opening moments of the service Father Craig (as he likes to be known) struck a horribly discordant note. Here's what he said:

> Terrible though it is to us, God grants the same freedom to cancer cells that he grants even to the most noble and virtuous of us.

As he spoke Nick's widow, Barbara, sat straight-backed and dignified in the front row with her two little boys. The coffin rested on its plinth a few yards from them, flowers on the top and colourful 'We love you, Daddy' stickers plastered on the side, incongruous in the sombre setting but touching the hearts of everyone there.

Barbara did not flinch at the vicar's words, but you could detect a gasp from others in the congregation. Partly it was the sheer insensitivity of the timing. If a middle-aged man with two small children and a wife who adored him has died a terrible death from cancer, his mourners do not want to be told at his funeral that God had specifically enabled the cells that killed him. They may believe in an all-powerful God who created every living thing, including cancer cells, or they may not. Either way they are hardly likely to be comforted by such a message at such a time.

There is also something absurd about the notion that cancer cells can choose what they do. They can't. They cause immense suffering and, ultimately, they can kill. But that's it. What they do not possess in any accepted sense of the word is 'freedom'. Freedom means choice.

I received a sharp lesson in that nearly twenty years ago when I interviewed Margaret Thatcher. I was the new boy on the *Today* programme, desperate to prove I was up to the job, and she was the prime minister at the height of her considerable powers. Think amateur lightweight boxer versus Muhammad Ali at his greatest and you begin to get some idea of the mismatch. I made it worse by trying to be too clever.

My not-so-cunning plan was to ask her, as a churchgoing Christian, what was the essence of Christianity. She would say something like 'love' or 'charity' and I would pounce. How could she talk of Christian charity when she was single-handedly responsible for three or four million people being out of work, their children starving in the gutters of our once-great nation? Naturally, she would be devastated and resign on the spot, and I would be the hero of a grateful nation. Except, of course, that she did not follow my plan.

Instead she snapped back one word: 'Choice!'

I hit the canvas. I had fallen into the classic interviewer's trap – worse, I had set the trap for myself – of deciding what the answer would be and having no Plan B. Perhaps if I'd had half an hour to think about it I would have produced a vaguely sensible follow-up question, but it doesn't work like that when you're doing a live interview with the toughest politician on the planet. You don't get half a minute – let alone half an hour – to think, and the audience knows instantly when you're in trouble.

Regular listeners are a bit like sharks. It is said that if there is only one molecule of blood in twenty-five million parts of water, a shark can smell it from half a mile away. Big deal. The shark has been around for thirteen million years so it should be pretty good at it. Interviewers like me have been around on Radio 4 for maybe thirty years, but a sharp listener can sniff our panic over the airwaves from a much greater distance – and they're every bit as scary as your average Great White.

Since the Thatcher débâcle I have had plenty of time to think. 'Free will' was the answer I got from Rowan Williams when I interviewed him on the morning after the Beslan massacre to the obvious question: why did God allow it to happen? I knew that was what he would say and I was better prepared for it. Not that it made much difference. I was not satisfied with it then and I'm not satisfied with it now. It's all very well to say that God gave us free will and therefore could not have stopped the terrorists in the action of butchering those children, but what freedom did the children have? Why were their mothers at the school gate denied their free will? The wish of every one was that her child's life be spared, but it did not happen. The terrorists had their way. They were able to exercise their free will. The children did not and could not. I returned to the subject in more general terms when I interviewed the Archbishop for my Radio 4 series. Here's how it went:

JH: Free will is fine for mature adults. Children have no free will. The murderer has the freedom but the victim doesn't.

RW: But isn't that the nature of the case? The free will of one person, of you or of me, affects others whatever we do. And I can't quite see how a universe could be constructed in which some people's free will was, if you like, guaranteed to be aborted at certain points so that it wouldn't damage others. When people talk about free will in relation to moral evil, I think what they're saying is something like this. God has made a universe in which conscious people emerge, people with decisions to make, with thoughts that can form their decisions. And because we don't live as isolated units, in little bubbles around the place, my thought, my action, impinges on yours. We're interconnected. Our freedom affects others.

Now what would it be like if we said, 'Okay, God makes that sort of world but there is some sort of cut-off point where the effect that my freedom has on other people is guaranteed not to make their life too difficult'? What's the cut-off point? That's where I think there's a rather stark choice. I think either you say that's the kind of world it is and go on reflecting in the light of God about it, try to make sense of it –

JH: – which is what you do . . .

RW: Which is what I do. Or do you say the whole notion of a God making a world with freedom in it just doesn't wash?

Well, if that really is the choice, I know what I say. It doesn't wash. How can it? Every devout Christian, Jew or Muslim I have ever spoken to believes in the value of prayer. If they did not, why would they pray? Why indulge in a pointless exercise? Of course, it might make you feel better, but the biggest element of prayer is asking God for something. In other words, it is asking God to intercede. And yet if he does intercede – in the case of the terrified mothers, for instance – he is thwarting someone's free will.

And there's another problem here. Christians believe in miracles. You cannot become a saint in the Roman Catholic Church unless it can be proved that you have performed a couple. If we are to believe the Bible on this, God was performing miracles all the time. In the Old Testament he was parting the Red Sea so that the people of Israel could escape. In the New Testament Jesus was producing a decent meal for a sizeable crowd from a couple of loaves and fishes or turning a jug of water into wine. I've always thought that to be a particularly funny sort of miracle, given the amount of suffering he would have come across every day. You'd have thought his power would be better used rescuing some poor soul from being tortured by his persecutors rather than delivering conjuring tricks to make a wedding party go with a swing. Still, I'm no theologian. But the Archbishop is. Here's how it went when I asked him to sort out this business of intervention and miracles.

RW: What all that presupposes is that God is in one bit of the room and there's — if you like — chaos in the other end of the room. God looks at his watch and decides at what point he's got to step in to sort it out. At the same time I think although the Bible uses such language, talks about miracles, there's already in the Bible a level of puzzlement about that. People are already asking, 'Well, if he does it there why doesn't he do it here?' And Jesus goes to his home town and he doesn't heal anybody. Why not?

JH: He picks the odd person here and there.

RW: Picks the odd person here and there. And I think the only way of making full sense of this is to go back to the basic questions. God isn't a person alongside other persons, a reality alongside other realities. There's someone on the other side of the room watching. God is the agency that's at work in everything and has set up the world in such a way that not only is evil possible, but moments are also possible where something breaks through of healing, of miracle. Why it breaks through here rather than there . . . we don't know the causes that make that possible.

JH: Something else we have to take on trust.

RW: On faith. On faith. What I'm trying to outline, and I know it's not a simple thought, is that God set up the universe in such a way that when certain causes come together, certain circumstances come together, more is possible than those immediately involved imagine, as if there's something that breaks through . . . because God has set up the conditions in which, in this situation rather than that, it happens. As I've sometimes put it, the membrane is thinner, his action is nearer the surface. And that may be because of human prayer, because of human holiness. Something more comes through than you might otherwise expect.

JH: John Fowles wrote, 'Freedom of will is the highest human good and it is impossible to have both that freedom and an intervening deity.' Isn't that the reality? It's either one or the other, isn't it?

RW: No, it's not, because if our freedom is the highest good and if that freedom is – as the Bible says – the image of God in us, then the full exercise of our freedom in holiness, in prayer, can allow something of God's action to come in with us. Not overriding our freedom but, if you like, working through it.

JH: But if we accept freedom of will, why do we pray? Why do you pray if you know that in the end God is not going to intervene, unless through a happy combination of circumstances, and then very rarely indeed? They prayed in Auschwitz.

RW: They prayed in Auschwitz, and they prayed, I imagine, for two reasons. One is

God is always to be praised, and the extraordinary thing is that they prayed in Auschwitz. That people felt that God's name was to
be honoured even there.

JH: Or they were in total despair and they had
nowhere else to go. That's the other explanation.

RW: And I think there's something in both of
them. But I don't think it's just about total
despair and having nowhere else to go. They
knew they were doomed. I think people who
prayed in Auschwitz – especially, you know,
Hasidic Orthodox Jews, going into the chambers praising God – whatever that's about, it's
not easy solutions, it's not rewards and success. They prayed because they had to do it,
God's name had to be honoured. That's one
reason. The other reason that I pray is so that
in my own attempt to be a loving focus on this
person, this problem, I may somehow make a
channel for God's action to come into the
situation. To what degree and with what effect
I won't know, but I've got to do it because I
believe that's one of the factors that might
make a difference.

I raised the question of prayer with the Chief
Rabbi. Why does he pray?

JS: I pray because prayer is my conversation with the voice within that is also the voice beyond.

JH: But is there, as Christians believe, a personal God who knows, spots when every sparrow falls, and knows when you get on your knees at ten o'clock in the evening?

JS: Yeah, of course.

JH: He's listening to you?

JS: God is listening to me in a much more direct way in Judaism than in Christianity, because in Christianity you pray through a son of God. In Judaism we talk directly.

JH: You cut out the middle man.

JS: We cut out the middle man, exactly so.

JH: And you believe he is listening to you?

JS: I have no doubt about it.

JH: Why does he not listen to the starving, to the sick, to the mother whose child is dying of cancer, to the people in Auschwitz?

JS: I've told you we do not live in the age of God the strategic intervener.

So we are back to this strange business of God listening to every prayer that is offered up – listening *directly*, according to the Chief Rabbi – and yet not bothering to intervene.

Obviously there may be many people who pray simply because it makes them feel better. It may be just a form of meditation that has a soothing effect on the soul. It may be purely an act of worship. Or it may be that, like me as a youngster, they're almost afraid to stop praying in case they reduce their chances of making it to heaven.

But believers use the word 'intercession' when they describe prayer. There can be only one interpretation of that. We intercede in order to bring about a particular result: if you pray on behalf of someone who's suffering, then clearly you are hoping God will listen and do something about it. I suggested to Sir Jonathan that one reason God appears to ignore our prayers might be that he's given up on us. He created the world and now, according to the literal meaning of free will, he's letting us get on with it. Here's how he answered that.

JS: He hasn't given up on us at all. When I found myself in a difficult situation and my late father did not intervene to help me out of it, I did not believe that my father didn't exist. Many years later I realised that he was teaching me that there are certain things I just have to learn for myself.

JH: But if you had asked your father to do something that was crucial to your survival, or if you'd asked your father to do something that might have prevented someone else suffering, you'd have expected him to respond and do everything he could.

JS: God always responds, not always as fast as we would like, not always in the way we would expect, but God does respond. There have been times, I've known them certainly, I've felt metaphorically as if I were drowning and God has stretched out his hand and saved me. I have no doubt about that whatsoever.

JH: Well, then, it takes me back to the question that I ask incessantly, possibly boringly. It's this. He did that for *you*. So why, unless he's a very discriminatory type of God, does he not do it for everyone who sincerely wants help? And, heaven knows, the mother whose child is dying sincerely wants help and may well be a person of great faith. Why choose Jonathan Sacks?

JS: John, I think we know enough about science today, we probably always did, to know that a physical universe without collision, destruction, cannot exist. I mean we are . . .

JH: God can create anything.

JS: . . . we are the dust of exploded stars. If those exploded stars had not exploded we wouldn't have an earth, and you and I wouldn't be here.

JH: And God made that happen?

JS: God places us in a context, a physical context in which there is birth and growth and decline and death.

JH: Twenty years ago I went up to Lockerbie on that terrible night when the Pan Am aircraft was blown up and the wreckage fell on Lockerbie. Some bits fell on houses and some bits fell on fields. The people who were in the houses were killed. And the thing that struck you walking around Lockerbie on that ghastly night was the entirely arbitrary nature of it. Number seventeen survived, number twenty-one did not survive. It seems to me that the God you're describing is a very arbitrary dispenser of justice and fairness.

JS: You're operating on the wrong image to begin with. God has set us in a physical world in which physical happenings can be random. There are faiths that do not believe that, but I do believe that it is a condition of physical existence. I cannot believe in God – the creator of the physical world – and at the same time have a view about the physical world that makes every phenomenon of physics or bio-chemistry, the intentional and interventionist act of a God who is doing everything. God is a remote cause and not a proximate cause. And if you find the randomness of that really challenging, then, John, you have more faith than you think you have. Because actually you want to believe in a just world, and that is the first movement of faith, the belief that what we do on this earth is not insignificant, that there is such a thing as a moral purpose to a universe. What I'm really trying to distinguish is the question 'Why did this happen?' For which I don't have an answer. And the question 'What then shall I do?' For which I have a very clear answer.

JH: Most scientists operate on the assumption that nothing can be accepted until it has been proven. There must be proof. And I've noticed reading what you've written that you have a huge respect for science . . .

JS: It's really good for describing *things*. It's not at all good at describing *people* . . .

JH: Well, all right. But scientists say that until an experiment can be repeated and repeated and repeated . . . until there is proof . . . we cannot accept it. That is exactly the opposite of the

184

message that you have been delivering to me
during this conversation. You're saying it
cannot be proven. None of it. We do not have
the answers. You must simply believe.

JS: What you're doing, John, is repeating the
same mistake which says religion doesn't fall
within the canons of science and therefore it
must be faulty. I'm saying you're using the
wrong metaphor, and that metaphor is not
accidental. It's been written into Western culture ever since the conversion of Constantine
to Christianity and the fact that the first
Christian texts were written in Greek and
therefore we are, as a famous American philosopher said, a series of footnotes to Plato. I
want you to think about faith not as a quasi-
or pseudo-scientific proposition, I want you to
think of it as a marriage. That's what happened at Mount Sinai. God married himself to
a people and a people married itself to God
and they agreed to go hand in hand.

I am intrigued by the notion that wanting to
believe in a just world means I have more faith
than I think. It is precisely because I believed what
I was told as a child about a loving, merciful and
just God that I now feel a sense of what I suppose

you might call betrayal. If I have learned anything in the years since I sat wide-eyed and wondering in church it is that, whatever else it may be, this is not a just world.

In a just world you would not have obesity as the biggest health problem for a third of the population and starvation as the biggest problem for another third. You would not have a pharmaceutical company spending millions to develop a slimming pill for pampered pets in the rich West while millions suffer for want of basic medicine in sub-Saharan Africa. You would not have millions of children dying a viciously painful death from malaria when the amount of money the United States spends on its military in one day would buy enough mosquito nets for every child in Africa for five years. And I wonder, when a child steps on a land mine or plays with a cluster bomb, why it is her life that is destroyed while those who sowed the loathsome harvest reap the gains. Where is the justice in all this? Why is it always the weakest who suffer the most and the powerful who prosper – usually at their expense?

Yes, of course these are naïve questions: the sort of thing you expect to hear in a fifth-form debating society rather than from an ageing, slightly world-weary hack who has been round the block more than once. But that does not invalidate them. Quite the opposite. It is when we stop asking the simple questions that humanity is at greatest risk. But the response of religion is essentially defeatist. It says this is the way the world works. This is the world we have created and it is we who have to deal with it. Fair enough. As a sceptic it's hard to argue with that. What it is not – in any sense of the word – is justice. Yet God is supposed to be the embodiment of justice. Nor is there any point in pretending this unjust world will ever change. It won't. It has been this way since history began and will always be this way. If we haven't learned that lesson by now, we never will.

There is no point in indulging in idealistic dreams of a different world in which nation speaks peace unto nation and we beat our swords into pruning hooks and stop spending countless billions on ever more clever methods of death and destruction. So let us not use the language of justice and a moral universe. A child born to a mother with Aids in a mosquito-infested mud hut will suffer. Forget about the scales of justice finely balanced. Think instead of a roulette wheel, calibrated so that only the very luckiest will win occasionally. And, once again, let's not swallow the stuff about God's 'gift'

187

of free will either. You and I may be able to choose
whether to add to global warming by using a patio
heater rather than putting on a sweater, but the
African widow with half a dozen hungry children
who will all suffer from the effect of climate
change has no choices. She just tries to survive.
She happened to be born in the wrong country. She
happened to be born poor.

Theists find various ways to reconcile the horror of reality with the promise of a just God – and
they always strike me as damned-if-you-do-and-
damned-if-you-don't defences. One of them goes
like this. Out of tragedy comes good. We may not
always be able to anticipate what that 'good' may
be or explain why the bad had to happen. The only
way we can ever understand the purpose behind
God's action is at the cost of our ceasing to be
humans and that can't happen because God would
never have created humans in the first place if we
could become divine. In short, says the Chief
Rabbi, we cannot seek to understand God's justice
– and neither should we try – but we *should* strive
to emulate his compassion.

I have two problems with that. One is the
obvious: it's simply too easy to say, 'We can't
understand so let's not make the effort.' And the
other is to ask: 'What compassion?'

Nor is it easy to see the justice behind God's decision to 'marry himself' to a people – the people of Israel. What's just about that? Why did he not marry himself to all the people everywhere? Why didn't he show himself to the whole world instead of appearing to Moses on Mount Sinai and leaving it to him to spread the message? It could hardly have been beyond his powers and it would have been much more efficient – not to mention humane. If we are to believe the Old Testament and its depictions of various slaughters, it would have meant saving the lives of an awful lot of men, women and children who happened not to have been 'chosen', or let into God's secret, and carried on worshipping the assorted gods their ancestors had worshipped before them.

We are told we must not take the Old Testament literally and we have to put the events described in the context of the times. But, to steal the language of Rowan Williams, that really won't wash. Either it is the word of God or it is not. It is the most extraordinary presumption for mere mortals – however brilliant they may be and however many centuries they may have spent studying and interpreting every word – to decide on God's behalf what is still 'relevant' and what is not. I may have missed it, but I can't recall the bit in the Bible or the Koran where God said something like, 'There will come a time when you will find most of the contents of these holy books either incomprehensible or simply barbaric, but don't worry about it because I'm sure you'll be able to sort it out. If there's anything that strikes you as unacceptable or just plain silly, feel free to ignore it and behave according to the bits that happen to be in keeping with the way you live at the time.'

The fact is that to decent people like Jonathan Sacks vast sections of the Old Testament must be anathema or – at the very least – deeply, profoundly embarrassing. The message could hardly be simpler: God chose the Jews and condemned to a sticky end all those who did not worship him. The Chief Rabbi will say that's nonsense. He points to God's declaration in Genesis, 'Let us make man in our image, in our likeness,' and says it is 'perhaps the most revolutionary in Western civilisation'. He also says that God's covenant with Noah was

> . . . the first covenant with all mankind through which God asks humanity to construct societies based on the rule of law, the sovereignty of justice and the non-negotiable dignity of human life.

That's as may be, but it seems a bit unnecessary to drown every living thing on the earth, apart from Noah, his family and animals, before getting round to the construction work.

So much for suffering, justice and free will. What about natural disasters? Why did a just and merciful God create a world of great beauty and plenty and make it such a dangerous place for so many people, with hurricanes, floods and droughts, earthquakes, tsunamis and volcanoes? In the wake of the Asian tsunami in December 2004 the Archbishop of Canterbury wrote:

> Every single random, accidental death is something that should upset a faith bound up with comfort and ready answers. Faced with the paralysing magnitude of a disaster like this, we naturally feel more deeply outraged – and also more deeply helpless.

But he concluded that there would be 'something odd' about expecting that God will constantly step in if things are getting dangerous. He went further:

> Wouldn't we feel something of a chill at the prospect of a God who deliberately plans a programme that involves a certain level of casualties?

Well, yes, but that raises two thoughts: why do there have to be any random casualties and why bother praying if God has no intention of 'stepping in'? For the Chief Rabbi, the simplest explanation is the one given by the twelfth-century sage Moses Maimonides – though 'explanation' is possibly stretching it a bit. Natural disasters, said Maimonides, have no explanation other than that God set life within the parameters of the physical. He put us in a physical world. Planets are formed, tectonic plates shift, earthquakes occur and sometimes innocent people die. To wish it were otherwise, says Sir Jonathan, is to wish in essence that we were not physical beings. But in that case, he says,

> We would not know pleasure, desire, achievement, freedom, virtue, creativity, vulnerability and love. We would be angels – God's computers, programmed to sing his praises.

But isn't that exactly what God demands of us? That we should sing his praises? Bear in mind that what the Old Testament is all about, when everything else is filtered out, is the worship of God. Not peace on earth. Not man's inhumanity to man. Not being kind to little old ladies and starving children and turning the other cheek and treating others as we ourselves would like to be treated. We get some of that in the New Testament – the Sermon on the Mount is a fairly decent guide to the way we should live our lives – but the God of the Old Testament seems to be a self-indulgent tyrant who demands to be worshipped. And if you don't worship him you're dead. Literally.

If you have any doubts about God's hunger for praise let's go back to the Ten Commandments. The first four are all about worshipping God and having no other idols or images and not taking his name in vain. And there is a warning for those who stray:

> I the Lord your God am a jealous God, punishing children for the iniquity of parents to the third and the fourth generation of those who reject me.

Once again, this is hardly the approach of a God who believes in justice. Why should a child be punished because his great-grandfather chose to worship a golden calf rather than the vengeful God of Abraham? Beats me. But we mustn't take the Old Testament literally, must we? Not even the Ten Commandments.

12

So, there was plenty to discuss in my interviews with Sacks, Williams and Ramadan. The argument was enjoyable – for me at any rate – but it was not the sole purpose of the interviews. They were meant to be an attempt to find out whether someone like me – a believer turned doubter – could be persuaded that there is a reason to return to belief.

Let's be selfish about this: if God does exist, then so does heaven – in some form or other. And it follows that believers have a much better chance of getting there than non-believers. So isn't it a sensible insurance policy to believe? Blaise Pascal evidently thought so when he wrote this three hundred and fifty years ago:

> God is, or He is not. But to which side shall we incline? Reason can decide nothing here . . . You have two things to lose . . . the true and the good . . . Let us weigh the gain and the loss in wager-

ing that God is. Let us estimate these two chances. If you gain, you gain all; if you lose, you lose nothing. Wager, then, without hesitation that He is.

That was the famous 'Pascal's Wager'. If you believe in God and you're right, the benefit is incalculable. If you believe and you're wrong, you've lost nothing. But if you *don't* believe and you're wrong . . . well, you've really blown it and you'll have the rest of eternity to regret staking your money on the wrong horse. And that's fine – except for one blindingly obvious problem. It rests on that word 'belief'.

You cannot *decide* to believe, in the way that you can decide which horse to put your fiver on in the three-thirty at Kempton Park. That's why the 'wager', or 'gambit', as it's sometimes known, is nothing of the sort. Neither can you *make* yourself believe. Of course you can fake it. You can tell the priest at your bedside as you lie dying that you've cancelled your subscription to *Atheist International* and would he please make free with the holy water. It's even possible that you might fool him into believing you're sincere. But you can't fool God – not if he has anything like the powers we're told he has. And you can't, of course, fool yourself.

Pascal was spot on in at least one important respect: 'Reason can decide nothing here.' But what if that's all you have? What if you're baffled by – and even a little envious of – those people who talk of 'seeing the light', or being 'born again', or having 'the truth revealed' to them? What if all you've got is reason and questions? In short, what if you're like me?

On the face of it, Judaism is the religion for us. The Chief Rabbi describes it as a 'religion of questions' and he quotes approvingly Isidore Rabi, who won the Nobel Prize for Physics. Rabi was asked why he became a scientist and this is what he said:

> My mother made me a scientist without ever knowing it. Every other child would come back from school and be asked, 'What did you learn today?' But my mother used to say, 'Izzy, did you ask a good question today?' That made the difference. Asking good questions made me into a scientist.

Well, good for Izzy, but there's a bit of a leap from becoming a scientist to becoming a believer and Sir Jonathan acknowledges as much when he quotes another man he admires enormously, the Hasidic master Rabbi Mendel of Kotzk. Mendel would ask his pupils, 'Where is God?' They would be a bit puzzled by that and answer, 'Is it not written that God fills the heavens and the earth?' The rabbi would tell them, 'No. God is where we let him in.' And that sounds fine too – except that, once again, it doesn't cater for doubters like me.

The question to which I returned over and over again in my Radio 4 interviews was this: what if you can't 'let him in'? What if you genuinely want to believe but you've never had any sort of signal from God that he exists, let alone a blinding revelation, and can't even manage to persuade yourself through rational argument that the whole God hypothesis stands up? I've always been perfectly prepared to 'let him in' but when I open the door there doesn't seem to be anyone there. So I asked the Chief Rabbi if he could help to introduce me to his God. Here's what he said:

> I'll tell you very simply, John. If I wanted to persuade you to become Jewish, the first thing I would do is take you to our old-age homes, to our schools, to the ways that we really do try and make life better for people here on earth in simple non-religious physical ways. If, at the end of the day, you said to me, 'What drives people to do that?' I'd say, 'Okay, let's now

move to the second stage,' and I'd show you our prayer book. And I would show you that three times a day we remind ourselves that God lifts the fallen, heals the sick and asks us to do what he does and become his partners. And then slowly we would move inward, and maybe you would never get to a point where you could say, 'Yeah, I really hear that presence speaking to me.' But I think you would have learned a little bit of a mystery that turned this very tiny people into people that made a disproportionate impact on the world.

I have come to know the Chief Rabbi reasonably well over the years. He is a good man, sincere and devout. He has a mischievous sense of humour and can see the absurdities of life. He is also very clever and immensely knowledgeable. But that answer was, from my narrow perspective, hopeless. I do not need persuading that there are many good Jews who try to make life better for people here on Earth. Nor do I need persuading of their piety, their devotion to God and the disproportionate impact they have made on the world. That last is self-evident but I cannot see what God has to do with it. For every religious Jew of my acquaintance I know half a dozen who do not believe in God, but it doesn't stop them being concerned, compassionate, decent, cultured people. As for 'partnership' with God, I'm baffled. Whatever else he may be, he's the boss. You can't be a partner, surely, with someone you are required to worship.

I talked about this to Tariq Ramadan too, and he wasn't particularly helpful either. All you have to do to become a Muslim (and therefore, presumably, gain the chance of access to paradise) is to recite twice in the presence of two witnesses, 'There is no God but Allah. Muhammad is the messenger of Allah.' That's it – in theory, at any rate. In practice, Ramadan told me, it 'depends on the state of your heart'. And he was obviously not convinced that my heart was in the right state. 'But let's assume,' I said, 'that I were capable of being persuaded, that I came to believe in God. In that case, what sort of God would I, as a Muslim, be worshipping?' He said:

First there is something which is the essential point, the oneness of God . . . the unity of God. The second point which is really important is that you cannot imagine how he is and you cannot define him. The only thing you can say about him is what he's saying about himself, so no image, no representation . . . There is a Chinese proverb that says when the wise man shows you the moon the foolish man is looking at the finger. And this is why we avoid representing any prophet because they were just men, messengers coming to show us the road towards the One.

As far as I'm concerned that's another big copout. You can't define God and all you know about him is what he says about himself – in other words, what he told Muhammad and is written in the Koran. And even that's not easy, because many Islamic scholars say it must be read in the original Arabic. You can see the logic in that. If it is the literal word of God and God spoke to Muhammad in Arabic (which he had to do because that was the only language Muhammad understood) any translation clearly cannot do it justice.

Neither does the Chinese proverb work very well. When the wise man points to the moon it is there – just where it has always been – and you really would be a fool if you couldn't see it. When the holy man points towards God there's nothing to see – which is why you end up looking at the finger. Yes, I know that's a very literal interpretation of what Ramadan meant, but either the proverb works or it doesn't. In this case it doesn't – at least, not for me.

But perhaps it's unreasonable to ask a Jew and a Muslim to help me believe in their religions. I was, after all, brought up as a Christian and have lived most of my life in a Christian culture. So what does the Archbishop of Canterbury have to say? I asked him why, if faith is a gift, it is denied to me and so many others. Here's how the conversation went:

RW: The gift of God is there for you and my longing would have to be that somehow or other that sense of being the object of God's loving concern comes alive. That's all I can pray for, all I can hope for. I don't believe that you're predestined, as it were, to un-faith – that God says, 'It's not much use wasting my time on Humphrys.' God, as the Bible says, stands at the door and knocks.

JH: What happens to me ultimately if I don't open that door?

RW: If you don't open the door you're not fully in the company of God. And it's your choice.

JH: And after death?

RW: What I'd love to think, of course, is that after death a possibly rather unusual experience might happen in which you'd say, 'Good God, I got it all wrong!'

JH: But it's too late then.

RW: No.

JH: After death?

RW: I think we continually have the choice of saying yes or no.

JH: So that death is not the end of us?

RW: Death is not the end of us. I think that's rather axiomatic for a religious believer.

JH: Quite so . . . but I said 'us' meaning us non-believers.

RW: Non-believers?

JH: Yes.

RW: God alone can judge how much of your resistance to God is culpable, to do with self-ishness, laziness of spirit, bloody-mindedness, and how much is just due to whatever it is that gets in the way. God alone can judge that. The willingness, the openness of the heart, even the wish to believe, God can work on that.

JH: Isn't the reality that ultimately you simply don't know? By definition you can't know.

RW: About your eternal destiny or about God?

JH: About any of it.

RW: I can be confident enough to say, 'This is where my life must be, this is what I hope I want to take risks for. This is as clear, as certain, as it gets.' And the relationship that I hope and trust I develop day by day in prayer deepens that confidence. I can't – either by argument or by magic – just transfer that history and that confidence into another person's mind. In other words I can't make someone else know that.

JH: But there's hope for me.

RW: Oh, yes, there's that. There's even love for you.

Well, if I got nothing else out of my interviews I did get that bit of comfort from the Archbishop: hope and love. He suggested I might go to heaven even if I don't believe. Which is a lovely thought – except that if you don't believe in God I'm not quite sure how you can believe in heaven. Then again, maybe you can go there without believing it exists. Who knows?

13

So the three wise men did not convert me. Their answers did not convince me. Conversion was never likely and perhaps they were the wrong answers. Or perhaps – and this is at least as likely – they were the wrong questions. My 'search' was genuine but was my approach misguided? All three accused me – some more politely than others – of exactly that. They had a point. I approached these three devout and learned men as though they were slightly dodgy politicians forced to defend the actions of an even more dodgy government:

- A government that promised the earth but failed to deliver.
- A government that favoured one group of people (the believers) over another group.
- A government that claimed to base its actions on the principles of justice for all, but actually allowed the most hideous injustices to rage unchecked.

- A government that promised to end suffering but appeared not to give a tinker's cuss about it.

The difference between a cleric and a politician is that the politician can say, 'We may not be up to much but at least we're better than the other parties. All you have to do is compare our record with theirs.' The cleric can say, 'You're better off with God than without.' What he can't do is point to a record for comparison. The clerics might have a great, vote-winning slogan: 'Believe in God and you'll go to heaven!' The problem is, they can't find anyone who's been there to prove it. And imagine how I would deal with a politician on *Today* who said, 'Look, I know there's not a shred of evidence for what I'm saying but you must have faith and believe it.' On balance, I don't think it would be terribly wise.

But there's another possibility. Perhaps they were the wrong interviewees. Many listeners had doubts about one or all of them. Why an archbishop? Why a chief rabbi? Why a Muslim academic? But if not them, who else? If you have questions about the law you ask a lawyer. It seems logical that if you have questions about God the obvious person to put them to is a cleric and, ideally, the man at the top of his particular tree. That was the approach we took at Radio 4 when we were setting up the series and it seemed a good idea at the time.

The comparison with another profession doesn't really work. If a lawyer has a problem in dealing with his client's complaint he has a massive body of case law and precedent to which he can refer. He will, one hopes, have dealt with similar cases before, and if he's any good, he will be able to predict the outcome of a particular course of action. He will also be able to advise the client on whether his interpretation of the law as it affects his own interests is accurate.

The cleric can't do any of that. For a start, there is no body of case law or precedent for him to refer to. Bishops and rabbis have only the Bible. That's it. It's true that countless millions of words have been written over the centuries by many wise men interpreting the words and the meaning of the Bible – indeed, my own interviewees have added to that vast body of work – but that's not the same thing. Clever Jewish scholars can spend years, lifetimes even, arguing over the meaning of a single sentence in the Old Testament and in the end failing to agree. They will enjoy the argument enormously. As the Chief Rabbi says, with great understatement, Judaism is an argumentative religion. His eyes shine with the pleasure of it when he tells you why a particular passage demonstrates a particular truth.

Even a theological ignoramus like me can have fun with this sort of thing. Some time ago I read with approval the following line in Proverbs (16:31):

> Grey hair is a crown of splendour; it is attained
> by a righteous life.

Well, exactly! That's what I've been telling people for donkey's years – or, at least, since my late twenties when the occasional white hair started appearing. Admittedly, it was always a little difficult trying to reconcile the sentiment with certain grey-headed psychopathic mass murderers from history, like Stalin, but there will always be exceptions that prove the rule. So I rested on my greying laurels. Or, at least, I did until I returned to the Bible for the purpose of this book and read the same passage again. Here's what it said:

> The hoary head is a crown of glory, if it be found
> in the way of righteousness.

No problem with 'crown of glory' – possibly a slight improvement on 'splendour' even – but how did 'if' creep into the verse? It blows the whole thing apart, doesn't it? Renders it meaningless. A grey head (or a 'hoary' head, whichever you prefer) might be a sign of a saint or . . . well . . . it might not. So, how to explain this assault on my increasingly fragile ego? It's perfectly simple. The 'if' verse is from the King James version of the Bible, first printed nearly four centuries ago. The other is from the New International Version, first published less than thirty years ago.

The question is, which should we believe? Presumably the New International. It was, as its preface informs us, 'a completely new translation of the Holy Bible made by over a hundred scholars working directly from the best available Hebrew, Aramaic and Greek texts'. And yet (and I write this reluctantly for obvious reasons) the modern version is barking mad. Believe me, I would love to lay claim to a righteous life on the basis of my grey thatch but even my long-dead doting mother would have trouble with that standard of proof of righteousness. She'd want a bit more than grey hair. I strongly suspect that what happened here was that the seventeenth-century translators produced a version that made at least a degree of sense. They supplied a meaning they suspected the original authors had probably intended but expressed badly. The twentieth-century academics who followed them stuck close to the literal translation.

If that's the case, then clearly the modern academics were right, but in all honesty I'm only guessing. How could I know? And that's the problem we sceptics have whenever we read the Bible – the Gospels as well as the Hebrew scriptures. What should we believe? The words that appear on the page in front of us or the interpretation placed on them by scholars some centuries or even millennia later? And if the latter, which scholars? Should we trust only those for whom the Bible is the word of God, or should we give some credence to agnostics or even atheists who claim to take a more rigorous approach because they have no axe to grind?

My silly little example from Proverbs is hardly likely to cause the likes of Sir Jonathan Sacks to tear at his splendid beard, abandon theology and take up macramé in sheer frustration, but it helps to illustrate what strikes me as an important point. If we are asking questions about the existence of God we cannot approach a cleric with the same expectations as a client might have when he approaches a lawyer. We can get an opinion, that's for sure. But that's all it will be. There are no acknowledged facts. And there is no judge to whom we can appeal for a ruling. Everything is up for grabs.

Which takes us back to the believer's core defence: if I could prove it, it wouldn't be faith.

PART FIVE
The Letters

14

I wonder if more than a handful of souls have been converted by reading the Bible. I can see that it might prove helpful if you're halfway there, but any stranger to the Abrahamic religions who happens to pick it up and leaf idly through its pages is hardly likely to say, 'That's it! The answer to all my questions!' They may enjoy the beauty of some of the writing (depending on which version they stumble upon) and they may be intrigued or even moved by the Gospel stories. They may be inspired by the extraordinary life and the hideous death of a patently good man. They may be impressed by the moral code offered by Moses or Jesus. But they are equally likely to be baffled by the bizarre nature of much of the content – the blood and gore of the Old Testament and the sheer savagery of this vengeful tyrant called God.

In other words the Bible, read by an agnostic, is as likely to fuel scepticism as it is to engender belief. It is an invaluable source of ammunition for atheists who want to attack their philosophical enemies. Like any other complex work of history or philosophy, the Bible has to be interpreted for the ignorant – and, for that matter, for the relatively well-informed.

So what about all the books that claim to do precisely that? There are an awful lot of them. I've lost count of the number I've read, skimmed, dipped into, stolen bits from or abandoned after the first two paragraphs of the blurb on the back cover. I have been impressed by some and seriously depressed or bored rigid by others – mostly those that quote great chunks of scripture to prove every point, apparently oblivious to the fact that the quotations work only for those who believe in the source. I have been angered and entertained, sometimes even amused. That last doesn't happen often. God may have a sense of humour, but I'm not sure it's shared by many who write about him.

Many are learned men and most are philosophers, theologians or academics of one kind or another. Some claim to have all the answers; a few admit they don't. They have left me a little better informed on some of the specifics, but none the wiser as far as the big picture is concerned.

So, where else to turn? Well, why not cut out the middle man and deal directly – if you'll pardon the

hateful and much overused word – with the con-
sumer? Which brings me to those letters I received
after *Humphrys in Search of God*. One of the first
things you learn as a broadcaster is that it takes a
lot to get the listener to send an email or phone the
BBC, let alone put pen to paper. They're much
more likely to turn off the radio in disgust than go
to the trouble of writing a letter, sticking a stamp
on the envelope and marching off to the postbox
with it. When you read in the papers that the BBC
switchboard has been 'swamped with calls from
angry viewers' you should bear in mind that it was
probably a few dozen. That's enough to create a
ripple. To get more than a few hundred is remarkable. To get thousands of letters suggests the
listeners really care.

I was delighted to get them, but slightly overwhelmed too. It's not easy trying to reply in a way
that does justice to thousands of decent people
who have gone to so much trouble either to share
their innermost thoughts with you or to save your
soul from eternal damnation. What they wrote has
been valuable for two reasons.

The YouGov survey on which I reported earlier
in this book provided a useful snapshot of the
nation's attitude to religion. What the letters offer
are some revealing insights into why people think

as they do. And they did something else for me on a more personal level.

It is easy for scepticism about religion to turn into hard-nosed cynicism. Clever atheists use their wit and learning to demolish the case for God – which is fair enough because that's the sort of thing academics do – but most go further. They make little effort to hide their disdain for those who believe in him. And I don't think that's either fair or reasonable. Perhaps, if they read my letters, they might have second thoughts and at least take a slightly more charitable view. But I doubt it. I suspect the only thing that might persuade them is if the Archangel Gabriel appeared in person in their kitchens, with Moses on one side and Jesus on the other, and re-enacted the Bible story from the burning bush to the resurrection. And even then they'd probably blame too much drink the night before.

Lest there be any confusion here, I am not suggesting the letters are the equivalent of a visitation from a shimmering angel, or that they removed all of my doubt – or even any of it. But one of the things they did for me was to prove yet again that a core element in the atheist polemic is mistaken. You do not have to be stupid to believe. Maybe it's me being a bit unfair now. Not even

Richard Dawkins, I imagine, would suggest that people like Rowan Williams and Jonathan Sacks are thick. But he does believe they're deluded, and the gap between being deluded and being stupid is not a million miles wide.

In *The God Delusion* Dawkins attacks Stephen Jay Gould, one of America's most respected evolutionary biologists, for having suggested that Darwinism is fully compatible with conventional religious beliefs. Not only did Dawkins rubbish Gould's argument – which, as I say, is fair enough – but he added, for good measure, 'I simply do not believe that Gould could have meant much of what he wrote.' That's not playing the ball, it's playing the man. And it's not fair. How can Dawkins or anyone else presume to know whether someone *means* what he writes?

As it happens, I have my own theory about the good professor. Richard Dawkins, it may surprise you to learn, does not mean what he writes either. He is actually a deeply religious man posing as an atheist who will one day enact his own public conversion in order to bring about a great religious revival. In the presence of television crews from around the world, he will sink to his knees in the courtyard of his Oxford college, clasp his hands together, raise his eyes to the heavens, praise the Lord and announce that he has been saved by Jesus. Just imagine the effect *that* will have on the religious debate in this country. There will be converts by the million. The great atheist repenteth of his sins. Hallelujah!

Or maybe not. On balance, he probably does mean every word he writes. In fact, I'm sure he does. I do not doubt either his intellect or his sincerity. Professor Dawkins should afford the same respect to others.

The problem is that he and his fellow militant atheists appear to believe they are superior to religious believers not only intellectually but even, in some bizarre way, morally. I can understand part of that. If I'm to be strictly honest, I suppose I'd have to admit that once I had lost my own faith I felt a bit superior. It is almost always much easier to make the case against something than for it and usually much more fun too. Playing devil's advocate is one of the reasons that presenting the *Today* programme is so enjoyable. But the response to my 'God' programmes had an effect on me.

Of course, some of the letters were a bit barmy, written by the sort of people you wouldn't necessarily want to have sitting next to you on a long train journey, but I suppose even foaming zealots have a right to be heard. Some people were downright rude. One or two reckoned it was just as well I didn't believe in God because I was such a horrible person he would refuse to let me through the pearly gates if I did. The fact is, they told me, I am destined for hell – and good riddance. And, no, not all of those who said that were politicians. Just a few.

Most of the letters, the vast majority, were written by sympathetic, intelligent people who have given their faith (or lack of it) a great deal of thought over the years and wanted to share their views and their experience.

Some were deeply moving. I was reduced almost to tears by the courage and resilience of people who had suffered appallingly: a few in Nazi Germany and even in the hell of Hitler's concentration camps; some from lifelong disabilities or endless battles with illness; many who had lost one or more of their children. A small minority were bitter and wanted to know: why me? Most were not. Older people especially seemed to accept their fate with resignation. They were more inclined to be grateful for the good things that had happened to them than to be angry at the bad. They did not parade their suffering or see themselves as martyrs or view their lives through the prism of their suffering. Rather, they accepted it, came to terms with it and emerged stronger.

One of the things reading these letters does – or should do – is remind younger people like me how relatively easy our own lives have been. One of my uncles – a lovely, funny man – was gassed in the trenches of the First World War and was never again able to sleep lying down. He suffered horribly and died an early death. I never heard him complain. All he worried about was what would happen to his profoundly disabled son, their only child, when he and his wife died.

Our own childhoods were not particularly easy, it's true. David Kynaston has written a fascinating book, *Austerity Britain*, in which he describes a nation after more than five years of war whose people were exhausted, undernourished and poorly dressed – mostly thanks to rationing. Even bread, which was freely available during the war years, was rationed and so was just about everything else. The bacon allowance was one ounce a week. My own house had an outdoor lavatory and we used the evening paper rather than enjoy the luxury of lavatory rolls, but at least we had running hot water. More than a third of all houses did not – let alone a bathroom or indoor lavatory.

None of this much mattered to us children – though the sweet ration was tiny and we'd have killed for new comics rather than the dog-eared second-hand ones shipped from the United States as ballast in cargo ships. It was our parents – working-class people – who suffered. They had lived through the nightmare of the war and now faced many more years of trying to bring up their children in a country where so many of their friends and neighbours seemed hungry, cold, dirty and depressed. Children are incredibly resilient and, anyway, we had never known anything different. And, though we did not know it at the time, our lives were to become much easier.

The young men of our generation would never face the horror of being forced to leave our families and fight in a foreign country, knowing that we might come home horribly injured or perhaps never return. We have so much to be thankful for, compared with our parents and their generation. We've been lucky. But it is we who complain most about our lot. Consumerism came to dominate our lives. We measured our hardship in material riches rather than the absence of war.

My letters reminded me powerfully that the generations who came before me accepted their fate with stoicism. Many found comfort in their faith and no one has the right to ridicule them for it. If their faith helped them through those dark days, their grief and suffering, we have no right to mock. For many it did all that and often much more. It is still helping them. For some, it *is* their lives. They simply cannot imagine living without God.

Dawkins and company may find this risible. They may scoff or even sneer. But if they do they should be ashamed of themselves. Believers have every right to be treated with respect.

The non-believers ranged from agnostics, who would like to believe and can't, to atheists, who were baffled by my 'search' and urged me to give it up. There were many who had lost their faith over the years. There were also pagans and spiritualists, Hindus and Buddhists, and quite a few who had their own idea of God, which they had fashioned to meet their own spiritual needs, plus some who left it quite literally until the last minute to turn to God.

Others travelled in the opposite direction. One man did a theology degree at Cambridge and contemplated ordination. His tutor, who went on to become the Bishop of Durham, talked him out of it – wisely, as it turned out. He described to me how his scepticism emerged early on. Indeed, he said, his study of theology – 'particularly the findings of Biblical criticism' – was a catalyst. He told me he 'differed profoundly' from me:

I now have no wish to rediscover a faith in a supreme being of any kind other than the notion of some cosmic force that started things off. My abandonment of theistic beliefs has come as an enormous release. I am now blissfully free from speculative theological dogma and the 'monumental wishful thinking' (Ludovic Kennedy's phrase) of a belief in an afterlife. So I hope you too will, in time, come to a contentment with your disbelief and enjoy the one life that we have without being encumbered with guilt or misgivings because you lack the blind faith that religious people regard as a necessary virtue. To compensate, I have found a happy home in Humanism and, since retirement, have gained much satisfaction from offering non-religious rites of passage to those who have no wish to be bombarded with the mumbo-jumbo of a religious ceremony that they cannot relate to.

Something similar came from a sound engineer in his sixties:

I too was given a religious upbringing – Methodist – but lost any belief I might have had as I grew up. A real turning point for me was the Aberfan disaster when a local minister of religion, standing at the top of a hill overlooking the stricken area and being interviewed for the TV news, said that it was God's will that this has happened. Did he influence the National Coal Board men who decided to overlook the presence of the stream I wonder . . .?

Nothing I see in the world today indicates that there could be a god. Take the difficulty the 'church' itself has in deciding on such simple matters as female clerics and homosexuals. Doesn't God speak to them at all? And give them the SAME advice?

Some were positively lyrical about their agnosticism:

We all have a spark of 'god' inside ourselves. Everybody has. We can feel it when we love and when we are happy . . . For me, 'god' is beauty, a smile, light reflecting on water, a spider stretching across her autumnal web . . . Why would you want to talk to 'god'? Why not just feel good? Why not just listen to 'god's' music? 'God' is easy. It's not crawling on your knees. That's not your style anyway, dear John Humphrys.

A retired GP told me he was brought up as a Christian by parents who were both elders of the Presbyterian Church but had been struggling with his 'long-lost faith'. He felt let down by my three interviewees because

> . . . none of them could explain why faith is so elusive. Why prayers for peace and reconciliation amongst the peoples of the world have remained unanswered for thousands of years. Why hope appears to be arbitrarily distributed or rationed . . . These three men – intellectuals, far more intelligent than I and (I suspect) you – all failed to persuade us that any of their Gods could be personal and loving, a God who is concerned and watches over each one of us.

A gay man, who conceded that he is prejudiced against the three religions because of their attitude to homosexuality, agreed with one of my questions: why is the 'gift' of faith vouchsafed to some but not others? But he wanted to turn the question on its head and ask: why do so many of us remain unconvinced?

> There is no doubt many do personally benefit from religious belief which in some respects may be a benefit to society, but this much seems self-explanatory. It does not constitute evidence of any supernatural or divine essence – external or internal. I have long thought of religion as a form of very ancient, emotional language based on a

'wish list', which may be part of the human condition in its development. Inevitably, perhaps, [it is] institutionalised and dressed up in ritual through being handed on and passed down from generation to generation down the centuries . . . religious belief as part of our heritage and philosophical quest for answers that can be made to fit all issues and which appear to convince huge numbers, but in fact become wide open to different interpretations – many of which conflict. As such, it is difficult to disentangle the need for a personal 'transcendence' with a need for spreading the word and hence for all religion to become deeply political, which is one of the reasons I have always avoided organised or collectivist religion especially.

One writer loved the sound of the Archbishop's voice ('so sonorous it makes me think of drinking exquisite Bellinis out of Baccarat crystal – not that I do that very often') but that was about all he enjoyed. The interviews, he said, were

. . . like being invited to what was promised as a superb feast, only to find that the food tasted of absolutely nothing . . . Like you I have this unfulfilled desire to believe in God – only at 77 years of age that desire takes on a certain added urgency . . . . My parents were really Victorians and came from stern Methodist stock, but my father left the valleys of south Wales to go to war in 1914. He lost for ever any religious beliefs he might have had on the Western Front.

There were many in that vein. I enjoyed a letter from a man in his late sixties whose main objection to established religions 'is all the doctrine and dogma, with concepts so archaic (e.g. the Blood of the Lamb) as to be far beyond my comprehension'. He wastes no time 'grappling with the stuff' but he does think about God. He spent much of his life sailing across the Atlantic in small boats and he described one trip:

We lost our steering and for seventeen days and nights were pretty much at the mercy of the ocean. Of course I found myself hoping we'd make it, and even hoping that some beneficial power would see us safely across. But I put this down in part to the majesty of those huge waves (they were not hostile, just indifferent to our fate), to the awesome beauty of the whole scene, and partly to my own very real fears.

Well, happily he made it across the Atlantic but he says he doesn't lose any sleep about 'not making it re the afterlife'. Rationally, he says, he doesn't see how there can be an afterlife for believers or non-believers, so 'we're all in the same boat', but he adds,

> I could be wrong, and if there *is* an afterlife (which would be quite a nice bonus for me after 69 wonderful years) and if there *is* a God, I really can't see him saying: 'You didn't believe in me, so it's the fiery furnace for you. Tough!' If he proves to be *that* vengeful and *that* mean, then I'd reply: 'Well you seem a sulky, petty sort of a God! I, a mere mortal, can conceive of a more exemplary and moral God than that. So where does that leave *you*, with your infinite wisdom, mercy and omniscience?'

He used a graphic image to describe how he sees the relationship between God (assuming he exists) and humans. He moved house many years ago, emptied an old fridge and found a cake tin with three iced buns stuffed at the back:

> They were covered with furry moulds, one pink, one blue and one yellow, and they were invading each other – presumably engaged in dreadful internecine warfare. They were living beings, albeit on a tiny scale, but had no awareness of

a world outside their tin, let alone the fridge. In contrast to them, I had been around the world, had seen the galaxies, had played Schubert and Beethoven in a piano trio, owned a copy of the *Encyclopaedia Britannica*. I felt like a God myself. I imagine, then, that if there *is* a God, a similar order of magnitude possibly exists between him and us. So how could he resent us not believing in him, when our knowledge is so limited?

A woman in her eighties told me she was born and brought up in the Church of England. When she was confirmed she expected that 'something numinous' would descend on her,

but of course it didn't happen . . . I draw a distinction between religion and spirituality. I believe this to be a spiritual universe, but I think religion is more often than not a distortion, invented through the centuries by priests for reasons of power over people. It seems to me that the relationship between spirituality and religion is that of a live butterfly sitting on a flower to that of a dead butterfly pinned to a board.

One listener, unimpressed by my questions and the answers, wanted me to do the series all over again with a different set. My questions, he said, failed at the first hurdle by not extracting from each of them their definition of God. This was his list.

1. What do you understand by God?
2. Does God know everything?
3. Does God know exactly what will befall each of us?
4. If knowing that, why does God knowingly allow some to be born into such suffering?
5. Who or what created God?
6. If God is self-created or has always existed, why can the same not also be said of the universe – thereby dispensing with God?
7. How does one distinguish between a true religion and a false one?
8. Can a true religion permit/condone stoning to death, or any death penalty? The differential treatment of men and women? The promise of heavenly reward for suicide attacks? The requirement that a church stands between man and his God? That sexual abstinence is a necessary precondition for serving God in some circumstances and so on?

233

9. What is the fate of all those who lead exemplary lives and yet do not believe in God?
10. What is the best way to rid permanently the planet of religious extremism?

I thought that was a pretty good stab at it. I wonder if he fancies a job . . .

An old colleague of mine at the BBC was not sure whether I had a 'real desire for a faith in God' or whether I was 'taking the part of that splendid character, the principled BBC agnostic asking the usual questions of the usual suspects'. He went on:

> I have always thought it quite ridiculous to expect someone to believe in God without having had any experience of him. Rather like telling someone to believe in bananas without ever tasting one.

A retired priest told me that for most of his forty years in the priesthood he had had a 'love/hate relationship' with the Church. It had not been helped by 'thin services, banal choruses, poor preaching and unfriendly people'. He admitted to being a prime candidate for the grumpy-old-man image. But he raised some more serious issues too. He has been taking daily offices even in his retirement and 'in recent months I have been ploughing through the early historical books of the Old Testament'. Here's how he described them:

> As God's people took over the land the instruction came from God to kill everything: men, women, children and cattle. What sort of God is this? Of course, with my theological training, I could explain it all away. But I put down my books and switch on Radio 4 to hear that Israel has attacked Lebanon with an overwhelming force which seems designed to destroy everything just as the Old Testament commands. There is the continuing disturbing violence in Iraq, the hostility towards Iran, the fears and threats of much of the Biblical lands in the Middle East. Some of it is fuelled by the Bible-believing co-religionists who believe that they are doing what God requires. When I get over my own desire to throttle those who believe and behave like that I just want to weep. What kind of God is this?

But he has tried to cling to his faith in God – 'sometimes with my fingertips alone' – and has come to some conclusions. The main one is that

> growing in a relationship with God who is revealed in Jesus helps me to understand that this God weeps with people like you and me over

the horrors that men perpetrate on one another. He not only gave us free will to accept or reject him but he gave us a set of instructions of how life can best be lived with each other.

He added this afterthought:

My starting point in your quest is not so much whether you believe in God but whether God believes in you. And the God I recognise does just that.

A Catholic who said she had 'been through periods when God has felt as close as my skin and endured times when I've clung on to nothing more than a thread of God about to snap' told me:

If your search for God is genuine, you can let go now. You've put in the effort, you've done the praying and pleading, so it may be time to relax . . . If you are to be given the gift of faith, you will receive it but at a time God chooses: maybe later, maybe on your death-bed. Simply put the matter aside now . . . No need to worry if faith never comes because what matters is the desire for it.

Another church minister said:

Aristotle says that if you want to be virtuous, you have to practise virtue. In the same way I think if you decide you want to have faith in God, at some point you just have to start practising it. How? It can only be by prayer. Getting answers to intellectual questions is not what we need.

There were many Christians who thought I had no right to ask my questions at all:

The God whom you are supposedly searching for won't be placed in your witness box to answer your questions. Why should he? He is not a genie to be whistled up at your command. If he is as great as Christians claim then he must be given the respect and reverence he deserves. If he is anything less than that, then he is surely not worth the bother.

And there were others who thought I was looking in the wrong place. One told me I might be better going to a drop-in centre for the homeless rather than to religious leaders:

Having 'broken free' from my fundamentalist induction into Christianity, I find that God is more to be found in people all over the place, including in some of my atheist friends, rather than in doctrines and philosophical arguments.

237

Some were disappointed that I spoke only to leaders of the monotheistic religions and thought I should have included others, Buddhism, for instance:

> Buddhists omit God because we can't know if there is one . . . Strange to bring a small child up by showing him a body, contorted in pain, impaled on a cross!

Another chided me for asking why God allows suffering but 'choosing the three religions that cannot answer this and not choosing those that can: Buddhism and Hinduism':

> We live many successive lives and evil actions in a *past* life have their effects in the present life. But we *see* only effects in this present life, and so God seems unjust but is not.

Another Buddhist wrote:

> The sole purpose of Buddhism is to understand the mind, what it is, where it comes from and where it fits into the scheme of things. They manage to avoid dogma. They also have the good sense to realise that there is no such thing as teaching — only learning. Swine, pearls, cast, don't and before, etc. . . . The moral codes are

not designed to appease some benevolent deity but are a means to an end and the mental and physical practices in the monasteries are basically interchangeable. The Buddhists have a more detailed explanation of creation, but they argue that if you do the practices you don't need a god. If heaven, paradise and Buddhahood are the same thing, they are probably right.

For the last fifty years the eighty-six-year-old writer of this letter has met her spiritual needs through transcendental meditation:

After doing it for a while I began to experience a power rushing through me. I have now learned this to be God . . . i.e. his Holy Spirit, the Life Force . . . I began to realise this presence was guiding me and 'telling' me what to do . . . a sudden idea dropping in unexpectedly, for instance, and it was always right and had the answer to my problem . . . not from thinking it out with my intellect, just an unexplained, sudden, inspirational idea straight from Him.

She told me she has nine 'amazing' children and eighteen grandchildren but lives alone now, is healthy and happy and 'never at a loss for something to do'. Not a bad advertisement, I'd have thought, for TM.

Other writers were succinct:

> Thanks for the programmes. We'll never find God listening to this bunch of snake-oil salesmen!

Well, maybe, but as I have said most of the listeners who wrote to me had already 'found God'.

16

Some people are impressed with God for what strike me as the most bizarre reasons. I was earnestly assured by one writer that God had performed a miracle at the time of the Kashmir earthquake in October 2005. It seems he held off the snows, which normally fall at that time, until the following January. As a result, much suffering was alleviated. One can't help wondering why, if God is prepared to intervene in that way, he didn't stop the earthquake happening in the first place. But I suppose we all see what we want to see.

For every sceptic there were dozens of believers who said they had been converted by a specific event or experience, many of them personal visitations of one kind or another. Indeed, on the evidence of these letters you might think at least half the population has been 'born again'. A more likely conclusion is that those who have had some kind of Damascene conversion are disproportionately keen to tell other people about it and share what they regard as their blessing – which is no doubt very kind of them but not always welcome. I must confess that I tend to be a bit suspicious of this whole thing. Too many of the 'born-agains' I've met have struck me as ever so slightly on the barmy side – but that may be because they've always scared me a bit.

Like many others, I suppose, I am wary of ostentatious displays of religious feelings. In the days when I went to church I was perfectly happy to shake hands with the vicar at the end of the service and exchange a few banal thoughts about his sermon. A friendly nod from the people on either side of me in the pew was fine too. But the idea of hugging total strangers to show that we were all brothers and sisters in Christ was a step too far.

Neither could I be doing with all that strange business of gazing up towards the heavens, stretching out my arms, palms facing upwards, apparently waiting for God to . . . to do what? I was never sure what was meant to happen. All I knew was that I felt distinctly queasy at the look of rapture on the faces of people I might have been sharing a joke with five minutes earlier. Most unsettling. And, of course, that was long before the phenomenon of the so-called 'Toronto Blessing', which brings me out in a cold sweat whenever I think about it.

It happened in January 1994 at an evangelical church of the more extreme charismatic persuasion in Toronto. Depending on which account you believe, some very strange things took place there. Worshippers were apparently consumed by the Holy Spirit, with the effect that many laughed hysterically, went into spasms, spoke in tongues and Lord knows what else. Some allegedly roared like lions or barked like dogs. Others wept and groaned and fell to the floor, shaking and trembling. One witness said it resembled a 'cross between a jungle and a farmyard'.

For a few years the church attracted a lot of attention and vast numbers of people went there to experience it for themselves and spread the message. It sounds to me like a pretty hefty case of self-induced mass hysteria, but I wasn't there at the time and maybe the Holy Spirit was. It might be nice to know what William Temple would have made of it. Temple, who died in 1944, is regarded by many as the greatest archbishop the Anglican Church has ever had. Here's what he once said: 'If you talk to God you are praying; if God talks to you, you have schizophrenia.'

Even so, many of my correspondents described experiences in which, they said, God had either talked to them or made his presence known in another way. A former legal secretary, who retrained as a teacher, had been brought up as a Christian, left the Church in her late teens and led what she called a 'pretty riotous' life. She wanted a church wedding but the pastor would not allow it unless she started to get involved in church affairs again. So she did. And then, one evening, when a visiting American pastor was preaching, she says this happened to her:

> I find it hard to put into words how it felt, but I can only say that I was suddenly aware of my own sinfulness in God's eyes . . . But then I felt as though a veil was being taken from my eyes and I saw all the radiant beauty of Jesus Christ and felt his immense love being poured into my heart to such an extent that I thought I would faint with the joy of it . . . That momentous event happened in 1989. I was changed for ever, as was my husband. It was the first time I'd seen him weep . . . I can never 'undo' my conversion because I have been changed inside.

Here's how another woman described her 'conversion':

> I felt that someone had put their arms around me and was loving me. I have never felt such love or

peace. I felt that I had come home – home to stay
. . . After a few moments I began to feel a strange
sensation in the stomach. It was like something
dancing inside me. It moved up into my mouth
and I began to laugh and an overwhelming joy
possessed me. I had received 'salvation' and was
free of the past.

There were many variations on that theme. A
ninety-one-year-old doctor (retired by now, I assume) told me she had been an atheist since her
student days but had 'come back into the fold'. She
was not one of those who'd had a conversion and
nor was she particularly impressed by the Bible. In
fact, she was more inclined to go with Porgy and
Bess:

> The things you are liable
> To read in the Bible,
> They ain't necessarily so.

Some years ago, though, she had read Victor
Hugo and his 'theory of the grotesque', which
makes the point that you can never really appreci-
ate good without having experienced evil.

The more I thought about it, the more I feel that
– despite all the savagery – this world is
so amazing, so wonderful that it can't be

gratuitous. It's just that we are not equipped intellectually to comprehend it. My father, not a particularly religious man, once leaned over and touched some snowdrops on the tea table. He said, to my surprise, 'Anyone who can look at a snowdrop and say there is no God is a fool.' And my merry old Welsh Mam, who all her life refused to take Communion, said on her deathbed aged 105: 'I will die in the faith of my fathers.'

She concluded her letter:

Though I can't pretend to understand it, I think now that I shall say the same.

There were also many claims of near-death experiences and minor miracles – an 'inoperable ganglion' disappearing overnight; a nurse whose broken arm healed when a devout patient laid her hand on it and prayed for her. A surprisingly large number of people clearly believe that miracles happen. God gets the praise for the good things:

People who pray for a miracle when a relative is told they have only days to live, and they survive and the doctors can find no trace of the cancer. People who are suddenly offered a new job from nowhere after months out of work and just before their house is repossessed. People who meet their life partner in an extraordinary 'coincidence' which should never have happened. In short, faith grows when we see and are willing to consider that God is working in the lives of people today. And it is through those people that His love starts to come to this world today even before Christ returns to fix the evils once and for all. It is in the charity workers on the frontline, the people who will give without thought for themselves, that the loving God is truly working today.

And Satan – very much alive and kicking in the minds of many listeners – gets the blame for the bad:

> The Bible makes clear that Satan – the ultimate source of evil – holds sway in the world at the moment. Whilst God is ultimately in charge, He is allowing Satan to have his way in this age. It's a little like a helicopter pilot who can see that two cars approaching a bend are about to collide head on, but does not do anything about it. God will heal all things, but in His own time.

Many writers make the point that Satan was 'created by God' but, as one woman put it,

> the free will he was given turned to pride and rebellion. When God ejected him from His pre-

sence, He took away his name Lucifer (light
bearer) – so he now roams the earth in rebellion
against God, without a name, causing the mayhem we see . . . innocent children being mas-
sacred, cancer, etc. Why God allows this to
continue is still something of a mystery.

A lot of writers told me about their own
personal tragedies. In a few cases it had turned
them against God, but mostly tragedy seemed to
have had the opposite effect. In almost every case
it had strengthened rather than weakened faith.
Scores had lost children. One man lost his mother
as well as his children in a car crash. Another, an
automotive engineer, watched his six-year-old
daughter die of leukaemia twenty-five years
ago and, like so many others, said a day never
passes when he does not miss her. He told me:
'At the time I thought I would die too.' But it did
not diminish his faith.

There was a similar letter from a woman whose
daughter had died. She wrote of 'the loneliness, the
awful heartache, the chasm she has left – even
stronger now than it was four years ago'. But she
says she has had 'extra help' and it comes from
God. She put it simply:

It was not God's fault. It was life.

A woman in her sixties was brought up a Christian but 'wrestled with doubt' for many years. She talked to a lot of people, read the work of various theologians and 'read the Gospels critically – and I mean critically'. Eventually she decided that 'on the balance of probabilities' Jesus was what he claimed to be. Then, nine years ago, her daughter died at the age of twenty-nine from asthma. Her faith, she said, 'hangs by a single thread'.

Another believer admitted that she was finding her faith 'a hard road to follow':

Eighteen months ago I lost my daughter and all three of my grandchildren. What do you do with pain like that? I do not know the reason for this happening in my life. Am I being punished? I don't know. I just know I have to trust that there is a purpose and a reason for this that I cannot as yet see.

There were many letters from people who were suffering from cancer or in remission. One had written to the *Daily Telegraph* to say she was 'looking for a heavenly Father to help me at this time'. That prompted this letter from a reader:

I have been down the cancer path twice and can empathise with her. However, I realised, some-

249

where in the mists of fear and despair, that maybe the 'heavenly Father' was an 'earthly father' who was present in the surgeon, oncologist, radiotherapist, nurses and everyone who surrounded me with care and hope.

A man, who was disabled from birth and has spent much of his life in hospital, was 'born into an unbelieving family, was sent to a school with an atheist foundation and was expected to follow my father into the Civil Service. He threatened to cut me off and disown me as his son when I told him I thought I was meant to be ordained.' But he went ahead anyway. He told me the four questions asked by Jean-Paul Sartre still stand:

1. Why is there something rather than nothing?
2. Why is it a cosmos and not a chaos?
3. How did life arise from the inanimate?
4. Where did man get his mannishness from?

He added:

If proof were possible faith would not be necessary.

That point was made by many:

Three times you asked for proof of God. I could equally ask for a proof that there is no God. However, that would seem to be as impossible as for a proof of 'love'. God, love, compassion, etc., are all spiritual entities and as such cannot be scientifically proven. They are experienced. Hence Christians have an experiential knowledge of God and all those virtues that make God's presence visible in the universe.

That bad things happen to good people is true. I see myself as a reasonably good person but, because I am human, I am not perfect and therefore am capable of doing bad things. Multiply this by a million and then I see an imperfect world. Nevertheless, amid the evils we witness there is also much more goodness. After all, the majority of people are not behind prison bars.

The distinction between doubt and lack of belief interested many people, such as this writer:

Doubt is not the opposite of faith. Doubt is faith struggling. Where God is concerned there must always be room for doubt. If there wasn't this room, we would be overwhelmed by God. Our freedom would be gone and we would be mere puppets who believed because we could do nothing else.

He reminded me of my visit to Iraq to report for the *Today* programme:

I dare say when you witnessed the dreadful
consequences of the war you also experienced
meaningful acts of unexpected kindness, or a
glimpse of truth or beauty or love like, say, a
mother's love for her child. They all made sense.
Although there is much happening in this world
that we cannot understand, there does seem to be
a loving mind behind some things and, if there is,
then this Mind must be behind everything.

And someone wanted to know, given my dis-
approval of the way the world works, what I
would change:

No doubt you would have aborted 9/11, the
tsunami and wars. But where would you stop?
Road and rail accidents? What about cancer?
Disease generally? And how about the housewife
who cuts her finger in the kitchen? Taken to a
logical conclusion it would make a totally un-
recognisable world and humans would be virtually automata, only able to do 'good' things.

A young man who described himself as an
engineering student drew a distinction between
faith and religion:

Religion is merely the organisation of people
who share the same faith. Its job is to give people

a place where they can meet, pray together, arrange pilgrimages, plan activities or introduce newcomers to their faith. In theory there should be nothing wrong with this. Most religions have good intentions and try to improve people. However, human nature means problems arise . . . In the end religions become vehicles for those seeking power and influence and it is in this way that religions end up doing evil things. But this is nothing to do with God or true believers.

A monk at Prinknash Abbey in Gloucestershire invited me to spend a weekend there:

Don't worry, we wouldn't try and convert you! You wouldn't have to stand up to your neck in water (old Celtic monasticism!) or eat dried up cabbage (with a little salt on feast days). We wouldn't even try to do a 'Monastery' on you (of the TV kind). But, in this funny, rundown old place, you might find a bit of peace and, who knows, possibly some answers that you extract from unwilling or prevaricating politicians but of the kind that you always sort of knew some-where in the back of your mind but until you were in certain circumstances, it didn't 'click' . . . if you follow my drift.

I did. He also addressed the question of why God allows suffering if he is 'good':

> In all religions there is a kind of process that feels like being smashed to pieces and being remade again, so it's not surprising that most people shy away from this kind of thing and, in a way, as St Teresa of Avila remarked: 'It's not surprising you have so few friends, O God: you treat them so badly!' This kind of thing can't be understood without some form of faith.

One writer managed to compare my 'failure to find God' with her disappointment over stroking a kangaroo. That was at the top of her wish list when she first went to Australia. Her hosts took her to a kangaroo sanctuary and she did it, but

> I was left with a sense of disappointment and still feel as if my dream remains unfulfilled. Although they were the right sort of general shape, ate the right things and jumped in the expected manner, and although everyone assured me that they were indeed kangaroos, they were not as I expected them to be. They were shorter, for one thing, and their coats, instead of consisting of short, rough, reddish-brown hair were soft and silky and a kind of grubby, sandy colour. I have stood in the

presence of a large number of kangaroos, yet something in my heart won't let me tick that item off my mental wish-list.

My questions, she said,

can never prove or disprove the existence of God, any more than me asking 'If that is a kangaroo, why isn't it seven feet tall?' can prove or disprove the existence of kangaroos. It appears not so much that you were unable to find incontrovertible proof of the existence of God but you feared finding the God that many people pointed you to. I would be very interested to know the 'character profile' of the God you were hoping to find (bearing in mind you already knew for certain He could not exist or, if He did, was taking a rather extended leave-of-absence!). It appears that you were seeking a being who would remove all problems, instantly arranging the world to suit the desires and requirements of each person on the planet – and of course zapping out of existence anyone who even considered upsetting the apple cart.

The realm in which our free will still exists is in our choice whether to worship God or not. In the physical world we are continually subject to forces and influences around us, from germs and cancers to terrorists and the tax-man. There are very few areas left in which we can exercise free choice, without someone else's free choice impinging on ours, but that one, final choice is the only one that really matters, the only one that can never be taken away or imposed upon us.

And a final thought from a man who was a schoolboy during the war and missed death on four separate occasions – by four seconds each time. First it was a German Heinkel that machine-gunned him as he ran for an air-raid shelter. Then he was on a train when a flying bomb (a V-1) blew up the track four seconds before it got there. The other two were also near misses from flying bombs. He says God saved his life each time.

When I read his letter I found it hard not to wonder what God had against all those poor souls who did not have his four seconds' advantage and got blown to bits. My own explanation, born out of my scepticism, is that he happened to be a very lucky young man. The fact that he narrowly missed death four times is no more proof that God was looking out for him than if it had happened once or forty times – or four hundred. If a coin tossed into the air comes down tails a hundred times the odds against it coming down tails again are still fifty-fifty. That's not theology, it's statistics. Unless, of course, the coin is weighted in some way.

Maybe God weighted the odds in my listener's favour. It seems perverse, but clearly that is what he believes. I don't. Neither do I believe that the various 'healings' or extraordinary events described by other listeners were miracles. Christians who believe in free will cannot have it both ways. Either God chooses to intervene or he does not. It is inconceivable that the God they believe in and describe in such loving detail will deliberately divert a flying bomb by a few hundred yards with the consequence that it blows apart one child rather than another. Or that he will destroy the cancer cells in the body of one perfectly decent human being yet allow them to multiply and ravage the body of another. And nor, I'm afraid, do I believe that God chooses to descend (in the form of the Holy Spirit) on one individual or group of individuals praying in a church in Toronto or anywhere else for that matter.

But it doesn't matter whether or not I believe it. Or whether you believe it. Or whether Richard Dawkins and every other atheist from here to whatever passes for eternity believes it. What matters is that *they* believe it. And what my mountain of letters makes clear is that they do. These are not, to borrow one correspondent's graphic phrase, snake-oil salesmen trying to sell the equivalent of a comb to a bald man. They are overwhelmingly sincere people who, one way or another, have found belief in God and that belief has changed their lives.

Why are some people capable of belief and others not? I hope these few extracts demonstrate even to the most intellectually arrogant of hard-line atheists that it is not a question of intelligence.

Some of these letter-writers may have been simple souls who were brought up in a particular religion and have never had the will or the wit to challenge it. Some may have been, for want of a better word, brainwashed by persuasive peddlers of hocus-pocus. But most of the writers strike me as intelligent, discriminating people who have given a lot of thought to their faith, asked a lot of questions and usually managed to satisfy their doubts. And yet many others have gone through that same process and remain unconvinced, unable to believe. For many of them the insurmountable barrier is the existence of so much evil in the world.

PART SIX

Conscience

17

In July 2006 Rahan Arshad, a thirty-six-year-old taxi driver, murdered his wife. He used a baseball bat, which he had bought a few days earlier, to beat her until she stopped breathing. Then he went upstairs, brought down one of his four small children, who were asleep in bed, and killed her too. And then he killed the other three in exactly the same way. Four times he went upstairs and each time he carried down a sleepy child. When they were all dead – mother and children – he left the house, took a taxi to the airport and flew to Thailand on holiday.

Those murders were not committed on the spur of the moment. There was no terrible rush of blood to the head, no hideous impulse to do something his disturbed mind could not resist. He was in total control of himself. He had planned everything to the last detail. Several members of the jury wept as the judge pronounced sentence. Arshad, he said, would spend the rest of his life in jail. He would never be freed on licence.

Let me recall a few more stories that have been in the news since I started thinking about this book.

- A young mother taking her small daughters for a walk on Christmas Day was attacked by a gang of thugs who stamped on her face until it was smashed beyond recognition. Her children hid behind a bush while their mother was savaged.

- A young black schoolboy, about to take his A levels and with a future full of hope, was stabbed to death for no other reason than the colour of his skin.

- A ten-year-old girl was left lying in the road by a driver whose car had smashed into her. A dozen motorists drove round her as she tried to crawl to the kerb. Even though a smashed bone in one of her legs had torn through the flesh and she was bleeding, clearly in agony, they did not stop to help. One motorist even paused for a closer look before driving on.

And our reaction to those stories? Horror and revulsion – mixed with fear for ourselves. Fear because, in the case of the young mother, it was a random attack. She might have been the mother of our own children. She had happened to be in the wrong place at the wrong time and it might have been any one of us instead. The schoolboy was killed by racists. We fear racism because it, too, threatens us all in one way or another.

The other reaction is sheer bafflement. How could they have done it? You and I may be incapable of murderous violence, but surely there could be no question of our refusing help to a suffering child. We would have stopped . . . wouldn't we?

Maybe. The fear of 'getting involved' is real. The famous words of the German pastor Martin Niemöller come to mind. He was referring to the cowardice of his fellow intellectuals who held their tongues when they should have been doing what he was doing: speaking out against the evils of the Nazis in the thirties:

> First they came for the Communists, and I didn't
>   speak up,
> because I wasn't a Communist.
> Then they came for the sick, the so-called
> incurables, and I didn't speak up,
> because I wasn't mentally ill.
> Then they came for the Jews, and I didn't speak
>   up,
> because I wasn't a Jew.
> Then they came for me, and by that time there

was no one left
to speak up for me.

'They' did not speak up for the simple reason
that they were afraid. Niemöller was too – as well
he might have been. The Gestapo did indeed come
for him. He spent seven years in the concentration
camps of Sachsenhausen and Dachau and it was
extraordinary that he survived.

Those who stayed silent must have imagined
what might happen to their families, imagined
their children being torn from their arms because
of something they had said or done, imagined
themselves in the Gestapo torture chambers. Pastor Niemöller was right as well as brave: in the
long run everyone suffers if we choose not to get
involved. Perhaps the world might have been
spared the most savage war in history if we
had, but our first reaction is almost always to
protect ourselves and our family.

At this point the Darwinian atheist will say: 'But
of course! We are the product of our genes.' Others
will argue that the existence of wickedness proves
there can be no God. And others, like Richard
Dawkins, will say it is irrelevant. Believers will,
mostly, argue that God 'allows' evil for much the
same reason that he 'allows' suffering: free will.

We get to choose how we behave – whether we follow God or the Devil. If God turned us all into good people we would be nothing more than puppets.

As you will have gathered by now, this is not a God I am able or willing to recognise – and I'm hardly alone in that. The contrast between claim and reality is too great, as far as many doubters are concerned. Either there is a God of love or there is not.

Theologians have developed the doctrine of theodicy, which is intended to 'justify the ways of God to men'. Theodicy vindicates divine providence in the face of evil – or, at least, that is what it is meant to do. But for those of us who take a less intellectual approach, an image of a man stained with the blood of his wife, carrying his own children downstairs one at a time to slaughter them, is infinitely more powerful than any number of profound doctrines produced by any number of brilliant theologians. The cry of a child resonates more than the elegant argument of a learned man.

But let's put aside for a moment the mystery of God's attitude to evil and take a more scientific approach. Psychiatrists and psychologists, sociologists and neurosurgeons argue endlessly among

themselves about why some of us become psychopaths or sociopaths and most of us do not. Neu-
rological research suggests that the answer lies in
the neocortex – the part of the brain that is
involved in controlling our impulses and conscious
thought. This is, literally, the grey matter, compared with the white matter of the cerebrum.

It is known that women have about 19 billion
neurons in the neocortex – the most important of
the brain cells – and men have about 24 billion. In
the last half-century scientists have learned an
enormous amount about the complex processes
that occur inside a single neuron and, in many
cases, how a network of neurons produces a
particular response – perhaps to danger or to
the way we understand a particular problem.
But what experts don't know still outweighs what
they do, and the really big question remains unanswered. In the words of Professor Eric Kandel,
one of the world's leading neuroscientists:

> The last frontier of the biological sciences – their
> ultimate challenge – is to understand the biological
> basis of consciousness and the mental processes by
> which we perceive, act, learn, and remember.

They do not know why our brains – which all
look pretty much the same – turn some of us

towards murder and some towards martyrdom. The American psychologist Professor Robert Hare has spent nearly forty years researching the dark world inhabited by psychopaths. Perhaps its most disturbing dimension is that when a psychopathic mass murderer is going about his grisly business he knows exactly how he is behaving and he has complete control over his actions. What he does not have is inhibitions. He may be intellectually aware that society operates according to a set of rules, but he has no emotional understanding of those rules. He has no conscience.

The notion of conscience seems to me to be central in the debate about the existence of God. Scientists have yet to identify a gene for it and I doubt they ever will. There's not even a helpful scientific definition. This is how the *Oxford English Dictionary* defines it:

> The internal recognition of the moral quality of one's motives and actions; the faculty or principle that pronounces upon the moral quality of one's actions or motives, approving the right and condemning the wrong.

I'm not much given, for obvious reasons, to quoting from the Old Testament, but I'd prefer a phrase used to describe the way God made his presence known to Elijah. He appeared not in the wind or the earthquake but in a 'still, small voice'. That captures the idea of conscience for me.

Over recent years the word itself has gone out of fashion in religious circles. The modern Christian view is that conscience is too self-centred and we must look outwards to God rather than inwards to ourselves. William Temple said the great aim of all true religion is to transfer the centre of interest from ourselves to God. But doubters, by definition, can't do that. What we are interested in is the argument over whether it is God who tells us what is right and wrong.

What believers and atheists agree on is that our actions are influenced by any number of factors: upbringing; environment; custom and tradition; fear of consequences. Both sides also acknowledge the presence of that still, small voice. But for believers its origin is divine and for atheists it is the voice of reason. As for me, it is difficult to understand the existence of conscience without accepting the existence of something beyond ourselves.

You can call that higher power God or Brahman or Allah or – as Socrates did – your own personal oracle. What you cannot do is dismiss it. It exists and it is unique to human beings. It is only humans that can be described as good or evil. We can anthropomorphise animals as much as we like – especially the higher primates – but in the end that's what they are: animals.

However distressing it may be to watch one group of chimpanzees attacking another because they fancy a nice chimp chop for dinner, we have to accept that that's the way it is. Chimps may be our closest relatives in terms of how much of our DNA they share, but they are still chimps and occasionally they kill and eat each other. That is normal chimp behaviour – neither good nor evil, just normal. When a human behaves in similar fashion, in what we like to call our civilised society, it is abnormal. We may faff about on the subject of evil and agonise endlessly over whether we should be condemning the sin rather than the sinner, whether we should understand more and condemn less, but the still, small voice tells us what is right and wrong.

Believers say this is because God made us special. Otherwise, according to William Lane Craig, we would be

just accidental by-products of nature which have evolved relatively recently from an infinitesimal speck of dust lost somewhere in a hostile and mindless universe and which are doomed to perish individually and collectively in a relatively short time.

The view of many Christians like Craig is that without God there is no absolute right and wrong that imposes itself on our conscience. If God does not exist, then objective moral values do not exist. If you deny the existence of God and take the atheist view, there is nothing really wrong with, for instance, raping someone. Over the course of human development we may have stopped doing it because it proved not to be 'socially advantageous', as Craig puts it, but that's different from saying it's wrong. The important word in all this is 'objective'. Atheists may well be able to develop a perfectly acceptable moral code but there is no objective way, without God, of distinguishing between good and evil. That is the theory.

I'm afraid it's rubbish. Are we seriously to believe that societies that might never have heard of a monotheistic god have proved incapable over the millennia of knowing the difference between right and wrong? If that is so, how did they manage to develop a moral code that is not very different from that of a Christian or Jewish society? Offhand I can't think of a single country – whatever its religion or lack of it – whose laws condone murder, theft or rape.

There may be social and political reasons for that – it's quite difficult to govern a country if everyone is rushing around murdering and raping everyone else, or stealing everything in sight – but that is only part of it. Most of us refrain from doing these things not because the law says we must but because we know they are wrong. We have known that ever since we became 'civilised'. That's the essence of being civilised – observing a set of rules and laws that reinforces a moral code respected by the overwhelming majority.

What is not 'civilised' is the way some of the great religious organisations have behaved and, in some cases, are still behaving. The Roman Catholic Church no longer tries to justify the appalling slaughter of the Crusades or the torturers of the Inquisition or the burning of 'witches'. It all happened a long time ago – but, remember, it was done in the name of God. And remember, too, what is still being done in God's name.

Sharia law is the product of profoundly religious men (*only* men, of course: women need not apply), who know for certain that they are carrying out the will of God. At its most extreme it calls for the killing of Muslims who decide to convert to another religion or who abandon their faith.

By any civilised standards many Sharia punishments are barbaric: for instance, the obscene spectacle of men and women accused of committing adultery being buried up to their necks and stoned to death. The most refined version stipulates the size of stones to be used. The smallest are thrown first and the largest saved for the final stages in case the victim is killed too quickly and dies before he or she has suffered enough. When the Taliban were in power in Afghanistan it was not uncommon for stonings to be carried out on football fields at half-time for the edification of fans. Once again, remember, this is done in the name of morality.

But we do not need the example of the loathsome Taliban to see where fundamentalist 'moral law' can lead in its most extreme manifestation. In the United States some Christians are so convinced of the evil of abortion that in certain states doctors who practise it go in fear of their lives – as well they might, given what has happened to some of their unfortunate colleagues. It's true that all religions have their fair share of crazies – no decent American Christian supports the murderous activities of the most extreme militants – but abortion is perhaps the most divisive issue in American politics, and those who condemn it see themselves as obeying an absolute moral law.

Perhaps we should turn the question on its head and ask whether *theists* are capable of drafting a moral code that *atheists* would agree with. On the basis of the code handed to Moses by God, the answer to that question would have to be no. Yes, there is plenty in the Ten Commandments that we could all – non-believers as well as believers – go along with. I don't know any atheists who positively approve of murder, theft, adultery or lying, for instance. They might engage in the odd spot of coveting occasionally – perhaps of their neighbours' wives, if not their asses – but I know plenty of Christians who transgress that commandment too. Jimmy Carter, the God-fearing president of the United States, caused a great stir in the Baptist chapels of the Deep South when he admitted in his guileless way to an interviewer that he had 'lusted in my heart'.

But surely any acceptable moral code would have to include a prohibition on slavery, which was considered entirely normal when the Old Testament was written and for thousands of years that followed. And what about racial discrimination? If you were not a Jew in the Old Testament, then God help you — not that he would: you were more likely to be put to the sword. Serious questions are raised, incidentally, about the attitude of Jesus towards other races. Biblical scholars point out that the first three Gospels report sayings of his that suggest he wanted to speak only to the Jews. According to one such saying, Gentiles were regarded as dogs, unfit to eat from the master's table.

In historical terms, discrimination in one form or another has been frowned upon only relatively recently. You will find no mention of it on the tablets of stone carried down the hillside by Moses.

Equally, any decent moral code that takes account of our more enlightened approach would put the torch to some of the rubbish spouted by certain fundamentalists. It would assert, among other things, that:

- Homosexuality is not a sin.
- It is not wrong to allow a woman to have an abortion so long as the rules set by society are observed.
- Parents should not force their daughters into marriage.

- Freedom of speech is a right – whatever offence may be caused by it – so long as it does not include incitement to violence.
- By the same token it is grotesque to call for the death of another human being because he may have insulted your religion.

The British philosopher Bertrand Russell – an atheist – suggested that ethics arise from the pressures of the community on the individual. But, he said, humans do not 'always instinctively feel the desires which are useful to the herd'. One of the devices the herd has come up with to make sure that the interest of the individual is in harmony with it is morality. Darwinists offer a number of reasons for the development of a moral law, for our feelings of empathy and pity, and for humans behaving in an altruistic way towards each other. You might think that Richard Dawkins, who coined the phrase 'the selfish gene' and wrote one of the definitive books on natural selection, would reject the notion of unselfish behaviour altogether, but it's not as simple as that.

Dawkins distinguishes between the selfish *gene* and the organism or the unit in which it functions. What genes do is make exact copies of themselves and 'compete in a pool of self-replicating entities'.

One of the ways they make sure they survive is by programming their organism to be 'selfish'. But there are different ways of being selfish. It might seem that you are behaving unselfishly when you care for your younger siblings or warn them of danger, but there's a lot of self-interest involved in that, too: they share the same genes and there is a close kinship. Another type of altruism is what Dawkins calls the you-scratch-my-back-and-I'll-scratch-yours variety in which animals of entirely different species help each other. There are some fascinating examples:

The bee needs nectar and the flower needs pollinating. Flowers can't fly so they pay bees, in the currency of nectar, for the hire of their wings. Birds called honeyguides can find bees' nests but can't break into them. Honey badgers (ratels) can break into the nests, but lack wings with which to search for them. The honeyguides lead the ratels (and sometimes men) to honey by a special, enticing flight, used for no other purpose. Both sides benefit from the transaction.

There are other reasons, say Darwinians, for animals to behave in an altruistic way towards each other. They do not include conscience. According to Dawkins, natural selection favours the rule of thumb – and rules of thumb sometimes 'misfire'. So a bird might, as a rule of thumb, automatically drop food into a little squawking thing with its beak wide open. That's fine if the little squawking thing is the bird's own offspring, but not so good if it's a cuckoo chick whose mother has heaved the incumbent eggs out of the nest. When that happens – and it happens a lot – it means the rule has misfired. In the logic of this Darwinian world it is but a small leap from one misfiring – small birds dropping worms into the beaks of the wrong chicks – to fully grown adults engaging in sex purely for gratification.

There was a time when the lives of humans were nasty, brutish and short, and their horizons were limited to the nearest cave or herd of woolly mammoths. They engaged in sex for procreation: it was vital to impregnate the women as quickly as possible and as often as possible to maintain the viability of the group. That, as you will have observed, is no longer necessary. It's true that in some countries there are worries about declining birth rates, but in most the problem is precisely the opposite.

The English economist Thomas Malthus has been ridiculed for warning in the eighteenth century that the world would starve because its population was increasing too quickly. He recommended – somewhat selfishly, given his own status in society – that the working class should practise sexual abstinence to deal with the problem. *Only* the working class, you will note.

His dire predictions have yet to be realised, but it may turn out that it was only his timing and his bizarre solution that were wrong. There are serious questions as to whether we can continue to feed a growing population – especially in the face of global warming. We in the rich West have been doing our bit, helped by the pill, to slow down population growth. But it hasn't stopped us copulating.

From this you and I might conclude three things:

1. Birds are programmed by their selfish genes to feed their offspring for the survival of their family and their species.
2. Birds are not very bright.
3. Human beings enjoy sex for the sake of sex even though . . .
4. . . . it's a pretty stupid thing to do in the long run.

In fact, Dawkins acknowledges that sexual desire is independent of the ultimate Darwinian pressure that drove it. He also recognises that when it is channelled through the conduits of linguistic culture it can emerge as great poetry and drama and is 'the driving force behind a large proportion of human ambition and struggle'. But much sexual lust, he says, 'constitutes a misfiring'. Even someone who knows nothing about Darwin and evolution can understand that. I suspect there's scarcely a soul alive who hasn't regretted some sort of sexual adventure – a misbegotten love affair based on nothing but lust or a one-night stand that seemed like a good idea at the time. We might not use the language of 'misfiring' but that word will do as well as any other.

It's when Dawkins takes his argument to the next stage that it really matters for the purpose of this book. He says there is no reason why the same 'misfiring' should not be true of 'the lust to be generous and compassionate'.

Sexual desire . . . is a strong urge which exists independently of its ultimate rationale. I am suggesting that the same is true of the urge to kindness – to altruism, to generosity, to empathy, to pity. In ancestral times we had the opportunity to be altruistic only towards close kin and potential reciprocators. Nowadays that restriction is no longer there, but the rule of thumb persists. Why would it not? It is just like sexual desire. We can no more help ourselves feeling pity when we see a weeping unfortunate (who is unrelated and unable to reciprocate) than we can help ourselves feeling lust for a member of the opposite sex who may be infertile or otherwise unable to reproduce. Both are misfiring, Darwinian mistakes: blessed, precious mistakes.

This strikes me as an extraordinary statement from a man like Richard Dawkins – fearless scourge of religion and champion of natural selection that he is. If he were himself a religious man his god would have to be Charles Darwin; his admiration and respect for one of the greatest scientists the world has ever known is perilously close to worship. When he wants to prove that God does not exist he almost invariably calls on Darwin to make his case – and a mighty powerful case it is too. But when he deals with something that seems to run counter to his argument (I almost wrote 'belief' instead of 'argument') he calls it a 'Darwinian mistake'. It may be a 'blessed and precious' mistake, but mistake it is. Or so he says. And this is not some peripheral matter we can brush to one side while we consider the bigger issue. This *is* the big issue. They don't come bigger. It gets to the very essence of what it is to be human.

Kindness, altruism, generosity, empathy and pity are the noblest of human virtues. To reduce them to a 'strong urge' and to put lust into the same category is to suggest that we can no more help ourselves feeling pity than we can help ourselves feeling sexual desire. Follow this thinking to its logical conclusion and you reduce human beings to the level of a marauding, oversexed chimpanzee.

Kindness and the other virtues make us what we are. By all means let us stand in awe of genius: of the music of Bach and Beethoven; the writing of Shakespeare; the paintings of Rembrandt; the architecture of our great cathedrals. They have enriched our lives beyond measure and the world would be a more wretched place without them. But a world without kindness, altruism, generosity, empathy and pity would be unimaginable. It is a world most of us would not wish to inhabit.

I can understand why an atheist who seeks every answer to the mysteries of life in the science of natural selection would want to reduce these virtues to something as basic as sexual desire. It helps satisfy the argument that, as Dawkins puts it, our moral sense is rooted deep in our Darwinian past, predating religion. On this argument, what humans do is respond to the most primitive of instincts – the instinct for gratification and, ultimately, the irresistible instinct to ensure the survival of the species. And that's all we do. To concede that something else is driving us, above all something that makes us choose to be good rather than bad, raises the difficult question: what might that 'something' be?

Clearly atheists cannot admit to the existence of a divine spark or to anything that might derive from a supernatural source. Some are happy to use the word 'transcendent', but mostly they look for more prosaic and provable explanations.

Dawkins and others are impressed by the work of a Harvard biologist, Marc Hauser, who conducted a series of experiments in which a set of hypothetical moral dilemmas was posed. The simplest involves a runaway train. You have to imagine someone standing next to a set of points by which she is able to divert the train on to a siding. If it carries on along the main line it will crush five people. The problem is that a man is trapped on the sidings, so the act of throwing the lever will condemn him to death. But if the lever is not thrown, five people will be killed.

There are variations on this theme. In one, five people are dying in a hospital, each of whom could be saved with a different organ transplant. There is a healthy man in the waiting room. If his organs were used he would die but the five would live. Should he be killed to save them?

Hauser used the Internet to put these hypothetical moral dilemmas to real people. What the answers to the questionnaires revealed was that when it came to making their judgement there was no statistically significant difference between atheists and religious believers. Ninety per cent said they would divert the train and save the five, and almost everyone said they would not force the healthy man to 'donate' his organs: it would be morally wrong to kill him even though others would live. I suspect you and I would have reached those same decisions. Dawkins uses the findings to conclude triumphantly that it is compatible with the view held by him and many other atheists: we do not need God in order to be good or evil.

That's fine. I agree. I'm sure you do too. And we did not need the Hauser experiment to prove it. Most ordinary, decent people will do what it takes to save lives but would recoil from the idea of forcing someone to give his own life. Most people lead their lives more or less in accordance with the moral codes adopted by the society in which they live. With some obvious exceptions, such as Sharia law, one would expect similar moral codes to apply across most societies and cultures. As I have said, the idea that people make the 'right' moral choices only if they go to the mosque on Fridays or the synagogue on Saturdays or the church on Sundays is plainly daft.

I'm much more interested in the question that arises from all of this: if there is no God, why should we be good? And on this crucial question the atheist response is as unconvincing as that of the fundamentalist religious believer.

The problem is that too many atheists have the irritating habit of setting up a series of straw men, then proceeding to demolish them. There is the notion, for instance, that if we stopped believing in God we would all become thieving, raping, murderous monsters. There may be a few evangelicals out there who believe that, but in my experience they're at the loonier end of the spectrum. Atheists are also fond of ridiculing the quote attributed to G. K. Chesterton:

When a man stops believing in God, he doesn't then believe nothing; he believes anything.

It's a clever little aphorism, whether Chesterton ever said it or not, but it's meaningless and every sensible person who gives it a moment's thought – believer or non-believer – can see it is meaningless.

In his fiery polemic *Letter to a Christian Nation* – which has been selling by the truckload – the American atheist Sam Smith produces statistics to suggest that people are more likely to be dangerous criminals if they are religious than if they're not. He has studied the political map of the United States and noted that the cities with the highest rates of violent crime tend to be in states where most people vote for the Republican Party. Those with lower rates are in states where most people vote Democrat. It is no secret, he observes, that in Republican states conservative Christians exercise an overwhelming political influence. From this he concludes that you are more likely to be burgled or murdered if you live in the most 'pious' states.

His analysis may or may not be accurate. His assumption – that there is a causal effect – is ludicrous. I'm no statistician, let alone a sociologist, but even I know that there are dozens of reasons why crime may be higher in one area than in another and why crime rates rise and fall over the years.

When I lived in New York in the early 1970s you did not go into certain areas of the city after dusk if you wanted to live to tell the tale. It was a very dangerous place. Happily, crime rates have fallen sharply over the years. Now, that may be – if we are to buy the Smith theory – because the people of New York have renounced their religious ways and embraced atheism. Or it may be because policing methods were changed and many more officers put on the beat. I'd go for the latter.

In the UK statistics show that most crime has fallen over the past ten years or so. You are less likely to be burgled than you were in the 1970s and 1980s, for instance, or have your car radio stolen. On the other hand, violent crime has risen and you are more likely to be mugged on the street. This is a pretty inconvenient set of statistics for Sam Smith. Which should we apply to his theory: the falling property crimes or the rising violent crimes? Let's try both.

Perhaps crimes against property have fallen because children have stopped going to Sunday school. If Smith is right, it is possible that the sweet young woman pretending to teach the kiddies about gentle Jesus was actually a prettier version of Fagin and was training her little gang of wide-eyed innocents to get out there and pick a pocket or two. Then again, perhaps the fall is connected to the fact that we have gone through a period of economic prosperity and high employment, when crimes against property historically fall. Hmm. Tricky to decide, really.

And what about the disturbing level of violent crime? Might that not be connected in some small way to the rise in the number of broken families, the growth of the drugs culture and so many disaffected young men wandering the streets looking for trouble? It could be, of course, that the violent young men are all born-again Christians who are striking a blow for Jesus when they wield their knives in dark alleys. Once again, it's a tough call, but I think I've made up my mind. I'd go for the economic and social explanations every time. Sorry, Sam.

18

Conscience acts as a brake to stop us doing bad things – things that might hurt our family or the wider society in which we live. You could argue, as many atheists do, that it is a natural development of the Darwinian evolutionary process. Remember, Dawkins argues that the 'selfish' gene is actually the entire organism, not just a single gene. So conscience is necessary for our family or our society to thrive. I have argued that it is more than that – that its existence is proof of something transcendent, beyond the material. So is great virtue, but it's a little more difficult to define.

We recognise wickedness when we see it. A man who murders his wife and children one after another is wicked. That – as the hideous business cliché has it – is a no-brainer. As for virtue, it is possible to do good things from the wrong motives. If someone gives lots of money to charity, that's good. If he makes a big song and dance of it and expects a knighthood in return, that's not so good. Motive is all.

The Roman Catholic Church – and most other people for that matter – regards Mother Teresa as a very good person. It has beatified her and she is on the way to canonisation. But Christopher Hitchens thinks she was more charlatan than saint. Her claim to sainthood is that she was a friend of the poor and devoted her life to helping them. Hitchens takes issue with that:

> She was not a friend of the poor. She was a friend of poverty. She said that suffering was a gift from God. She spent her life opposing the only known cure for poverty, which is the empowerment of women and the emancipation of them from a livestock version of compulsory reproduction. And she was a friend to the worst of the rich, taking misappropriated money from the atrocious Duvalier family in Haiti, whose rule she praised in return . . . Where did that money, and all the other donations, go? The primitive hospice in Calcutta was as run down when she died as it always had been – she preferred California clinics when she got sick herself – and her order always refused to publish any audit. But we have her own claim that she opened 500 convents in

more than a hundred countries, all bearing the name of her own order. Excuse me, but this is modesty and humility?

Hitchens has said it was by talking to her that he discovered that she was not working to alleviate poverty but 'she was working to expand the number of Catholics'. She herself said, 'I'm not a social worker. I don't do it for this reason. I do it for Christ. I do it for the Church.'

Well, maybe Hitchens is right and millions of other people are wrong about Mother Teresa. He's certainly right about the general principle: real virtue must rest not on outcome but intention. The man who jumps into a raging sea to rescue a stranger without regard to his own safety and dies in the attempt achieves nothing, but his action was noble. The 'celebrity' who succeeds in pulling a child from a pond and rushes off to tell the papers about it may have been more effective but was obviously less praiseworthy. Let me cite a few cases that demonstrate, for me at least, real virtue.

On a spring morning in 2007 Virginia Tech became the latest American college to fall victim to a deranged young man with a persecution mania, a collection of guns and enough ammunition to kill thirty-three people and wound many more. Almost all of them were young students. It is hard to forget the image of the killer, Cho Seung Hui, posing in front of his video camera, reading his insane manifesto, rampaging around the college shooting everyone he came across.

But another image from that terrible morning sticks in my memory. It is of a man who sacrificed his life to save his students – a seventy-six-year-old maths professor called Liviu Librescu. Mr Librescu might have escaped, as so many did. He heard the gunfire getting ever closer to his own classroom. He could have run. Instead, he stayed and held shut the classroom door so that his students could scramble to safety through the windows. He knew that would almost certainly mean his own death but he did it anyway.

Of course, it's possible that Mr Librescu was acting purely mechanically. Some primitive instinct over which he had no control might have been telling him, 'You're an old man and your life is coming to an end, so it is in the interest of your species that you protect the young.' But if that were so, would we not all act in the same way? The fact is, we don't. We might well sacrifice our lives to protect our own children – but to protect others? Mr Librescu did that.

Lisa Potts did something similar. When a madman with a two-foot-long machete attacked a group of eighteen small children enjoying a teddy bears' picnic at their infants' school in Wolverhampton in the summer of 1996 she was looking after them. She did not run away in fear of her life. She put herself between the madman and the children. He did his best to hack her to death, viciously slashing at her head and back. He almost severed her right arm. But she stood her ground and none of the children were killed. She was eighteen.

You might acknowledge that she was brave, but point out that physical courage is not necessarily proof of virtue: some soldiers show great courage on the battlefield and behave like thugs when they get back to their barracks. You might even say Lisa Potts was afraid that if she ran away she would be branded a coward. Or perhaps she was seized by an impulse over which she had no control and her example proves nothing. Again, you could say she was acting out of some Darwinian instinct to save the future generation of children for the continuation of the species, that she was behaving like any animal protecting its young. But if that is so, wouldn't we all behave in the same way in similar circumstances?

The fact is, she was an exceptional young woman who was prepared to sacrifice her own life to save others and was awarded the George Cross – the highest honour British society can confer on a civilian for courage and, by definition, something out of the ordinary. The way Lisa Potts conducted herself during the months of painful surgery and suffering that followed the attack – the uncomplaining, quiet modesty and humility – made her all the more remarkable.

Is it relevant that Lisa Potts was a Christian? Did she have a propensity to be good because of her religion or might it have been the other way round? Are 'good' people more likely to believe in God or does belief make you good? Literature offers many examples of selfless behaviour. In *A Tale of Two Cities* Sydney Carton deliberately changes places with his French lookalike Charles Darnay and takes his place in front of the execution squad. He says:

> It is a far, far better thing that I do, than I have ever done; it is a far, far better rest that I go to, than I have ever known.

This seems to be pure altruism. Carton gave his life so that Lucie Manette could have a future with the man she loved. Again, there is a cynical interpretation: he knew he was going to heaven, and this was merely speeding up the process. You could even interpret it as a selfish act. Remember that Lewis Wolpert's son told him, after he had been 'born again', that he envied those who were close to death because they would be in heaven sooner than him.

Carton was the product of Charles Dickens's fertile imagination. Irena Sendlerova was real.

You will have heard of Oskar Schindler because he has been made famous by a book and a film about him. He saved many Jews from the Nazis. Sendlerova saved many more – 2,500 children and babies – and her awe-inspiring bravery has gone unrecognised until relatively recently. By the time you read these words it is possible that she will have been awarded the Nobel Peace Prize. There can scarcely be a worthier winner.

She was a social worker in Poland when the Nazis invaded and methodically set about trying to murder every Jewish man, woman and child. In 1940 they established the infamous Warsaw Ghetto, isolating the 380,000 Jews in the city. The intention was that all those who did not die of starvation or disease, or were too sick, old or young to work, would be shipped off to the concentration camps.

Mrs Sendlerova, who was not yet thirty years old, organised a small group of social workers to smuggle Jewish children to safety. Because she worked in the city's health department, she had permission to enter the ghetto. She and her colleagues employed every tactic they could think of to smuggle out children and babies. They hid them in ambulances, led them through the sewage system deep underground (imagine the horror of that), wheeled them out on trolleys or in wheelbarrows hidden in cardboard boxes or covered with rubbish. And she wrote the name of every child on cigarette papers – not once but twice, to be sure. The papers were sealed in old bottles and buried in gardens so that one day, she hoped, the children could be identified and reunited with their families. Mostly that hope would not be realised. Almost all of their parents were murdered in the death camps. But the children lived, smuggled out of the city through networks organised by other very brave people.

What Irena Sendlerova did was good: pure and unalloyed good. She was an intelligent woman and must have known that all she stood to gain from her actions was a life lived in fear and the near certainty of her own brutal death. Every hour of every day for the better part of two years she must have been waiting for the hammering on her door, the gun rammed into her spine and the Gestapo torture that would follow. She did not know the children she saved. She did not share their religion or their race. They were strangers to her in every sense, but she did it anyway. Not just once: this was no impulsive act of mercy. It was not like seeing a child fall in a lake and jumping in to rescue her – or even stepping into the path of a machete-swinging madman to save the children in your care. This was calculated, repeated over and over again.

With every child spirited out of the hell of the Warsaw Ghetto, rescued from the unimaginable horror of the Nazi death camps, she moved a step closer to her own capture. And in the end – as it was bound to – it happened. She was caught by the Gestapo and savagely beaten, both legs and feet broken, then taken away to be murdered. Mercifully, she was saved by partisans and lived a full life. And not once did she boast about what she had done or demand recognition. Her awe-inspiring story remained virtually untold until she was an old woman, almost half a century after the war had ended. In an interview at the age of ninety-seven she said:

I was brought up to believe that a person must be
rescued when drowning, regardless of religion
and nationality. The term 'hero' irritates me
greatly. The opposite is true. I continue to have
pangs of conscience that I did so little.

Most of us are brought up to believe that suffering
should be alleviated. Only the truly exceptional
have the strength and humanity to do what Mrs
Sendlerova did. But her story is relevant because of
what drove her to do it. It may be scientifically
plausible to talk of primitive 'urges' and of 'mis-
firings' and of 'Darwinian mistakes'. It may be
that she saved the lives of 2,500 children because,
as Dawkins might put it, she simply 'could not
help herself'.

But I don't believe that. I believe she did it
because she was a good woman blessed with a
capacity for pure, unselfish love and a conscience
that would not allow her to behave in any other
way. She was a truly virtuous woman. And it
raises that troubling question: if we dismiss all
notion of a divine spark why did she do it?

There are, as far as I know, no photographs of Irena
Sendlerova going about her heroic work in the

Warsaw Ghetto. That is hardly surprising: the risk of taking them and hiding them would have been much too great. There are, though, many photographs that bear witness to the foul nature of the ghetto. One has stayed in my mind since I first saw it many years ago. It shows small children being herded out of their homes, their thin faces and hollow eyes betraying the months or, perhaps, years of slow starvation and gnawing, spirit-sapping fear. Their hands are held up in the air, as though they are dangerous gangsters who have been rounded up by officers of the law instead of pathetic, skinny children with dark-ringed eyes who look barely capable of putting one foot in front of another. On one side of the picture are their terrified mothers and on the other grinning Nazi soldiers with machine-guns held loosely, pointed in the direction of their captives. It is impossible to look at that picture without wondering how the soldiers could do such terrible work – but the explanation is quite simple.

It is the first rule of war that the enemy be dehumanised. How else could someone tear a child from the arms of a fellow human being and send that child to her death? How else could decent men drop incendiary bombs on a city knowing that they would burn the flesh from every living soul beneath them?

Military commanders have known this since warfare began. Genghis Khan was no different from a commander on the Western Front in the First World War. The most senior officers panicked when British and German soldiers left their trenches in 1914, declared their own Christmas 'truce' and sang carols, played football and even swapped presents. A man will plunge a bayonet into the chest of a stranger – the savage, faceless enemy – more readily than he will into that of another human being whose hand he has shaken, whose eyes he has looked into to discover that he is just another man – like him. The officers ordered the men back into their trenches and directed the senseless slaughter to continue. The battle of the Somme was the bloodiest in the history of warfare. The British alone lost twenty thousand men in one morning. By the end of the offensive there were more than a million casualties. The Germans had been driven back only a few miles.

As for that photograph, it contains no blood and gore, no shattered bodies half buried in mud. Just menace. It demonstrates the ultimate extremes of human behaviour, the unbearable suffering of the innocent and the casual wickedness of their tormentors. Those jackbooted men probably had children of their own but still they played their part in an act of monstrous evil. That is because to them the children were not children. They were Jews. And Jews were not human beings like them and their loved ones. They were little better than animals who must be eliminated.

So, perhaps that's it. Perhaps the Darwinian explanation will, after all, suffice. War is about winning. It is, by definition, a battle for survival. But that won't quite do, will it? And one of the reasons it won't do is that in the background of that photograph, where the camera could not see, there was a woman called Irena Sendlerova and her troublesome conscience. She was obeying a moral law that was higher than any other instinct, and more powerful than her fear of the Nazis.

At about the same time, a few hundred miles away, C. S. Lewis was serving as an air-raid warden, doing what he could to help the people of London cope with the threat from Hitler. At the height of the blitz, four hundred bombers a night pounded London, turning homes into rubble and terrifying the population. Twenty-three years earlier, as a young man, Lewis had served in the trenches during the First World War – which was supposed to end all wars. One way and another, he had seen more than his share of suffering. It was between the two wars that he became a Christian. 'I gave in and admitted that God was God,' was how he put it.

He gave a series of talks to men in the RAF about how Christians could deal with the problems of suffering, pain and evil. Many in his audience were doing to the Germans what the Luftwaffe was doing to the British. The talks were broadcast on the BBC and Lewis turned them into one of his most popular books on religion: *Mere Christianity*. When he talked about conscience and about the moral law (or, as he often described it, the 'rule of decent behaviour') he received many letters from listeners.

Some questioned the existence of a merciful God, let alone 'decent behaviour' in the middle of so much killing and suffering, and suggested that the moral law was nothing more than herd instinct, developed in the same way as other instincts, such as mother love or the sexual drive. Lewis had some sympathy with that argument. He acknowledged that feeling a desire or an urge to help might well relate to the herd instinct. He could almost have been speaking the language of Dawkins half a century later. Almost — but not quite. Because here is how he went on:

Feeling a desire to help is quite different from feeling that you *ought* to help whether you want to or not. Supposing you hear a cry for help from a man in danger. You will probably feel two desires: one desire to give help, due to your herd instinct; the other a desire to keep out of danger, due to the instinct for self-preservation. But you will find inside you, in addition to these two impulses, a third thing which tells you that you ought to follow the impulse to help and suppress the impulse to run away. This thing that judges between the two instincts, that decides which should be encouraged, cannot itself be either of them. You might as well say that the sheet of music which tells you, at a given moment, to play one note on the piano and not another, is itself one of the notes on the keyboard. The moral law tells us the tune we have to play. Our instincts are merely the keys.

This causes a problem for the atheist Darwinists. The herd instinct is a natural response – but so is that for self-preservation. It might be a physical thing: whether to help a woman being tormented by a gang of yobs in a train carriage or, at the opposite end of the scale, whether to save Jewish children from the Nazis. It might even be a purely material choice: whether to give money to the beggar in the street or make a donation to a deserving charity. In every case, both instincts apply. By standing up to the yobs you make the society in which you have to live a little bit safer. By helping educate orphans in Africa you make it a tiny bit less likely that they will end up as penniless illegal immigrants threatening your own rich country's prosperity or even security. But in every case you might also jeopardise your own position. One of the yobs might stick a knife in your stomach. The money you give away might have been used for your own children. What happens when the two instincts are in conflict?

Lewis makes the obvious point that if there is nothing else in our minds except those two instincts, the stronger of the two must win. By any Darwinian measure the stronger is bound to be self-preservation. But that reckons without the sheet of music: the moral law. Our conscience. Lewis observes that when we are most conscious of the moral law 'it usually seems to be telling us to side with the weaker of the two impulses'. We may not, in the end, do the right thing, but we know what the right thing is.

But perhaps we think in terms of right and wrong only because that is what we have been taught. Maybe the moral law is little more than a social convention, something we absorb with our mothers' milk, pick up at school, learn from different teachers as we go through life. Maybe it is no more than a human invention. If that really is the case, we should be able to change it. We can change most rules. We British could decide next week to start driving on the right-hand side of the road. We could even – though, admittedly, this might lead to serious social unrest because it would demolish the myth of male superiority over females – abolish the offside rule in football.

But we cannot change the moral law. Lewis offers the multiplication tables (remember: this was sixty years ago, before every child had a computer or calculator) to make this point. It's perfectly obvious that the tables were invented by humans and taught by teachers. But that doesn't make them 'conventions'. Twice times two will always be four – even if someone decides to change the rule. It is true wherever you live and whatever century you happen to have lived or live in. It is immutable. But can we really say the same about the moral law? Consider this short list:

- We burned heretics at the stake.
- Slavery was regarded as a perfectly acceptable way to make money.

- Children were sent up chimneys to die excruciatingly painful deaths from the soot they breathed.
- Soldiers suffering from shell shock were shot at dawn.
- Fathers were hanged for stealing bread to give to their children.
- Homosexuals were imprisoned – or worse.

All those foul practices and many, many more have been ended in virtually every civilised country in the world. Doesn't that suggest that the moral law really is no more than a social convention – something that changes with the passing of time?

On the face of it, yes, but look again at that list. In every case the laws were changed and the practices ended because they were deemed to be wrong. Morally wrong. If that seems a statement of the blindingly obvious, it's meant to be.

Whenever mature democracies have had to choose between laws and practices that you or I, in the quiet of our own consciences, know to be wrong and those that we know to be right, we have chosen the right. It is true that we have usually been led by reformers of exceptional moral courage, such as William Wilberforce or Albert

Schweitzer, and it is also true that sometimes there has been resistance. But in the end we have done the right thing. And it has worked like a ratchet. We have moved in only one direction. It is inconceivable that we will ever again treat children as we did a couple of centuries ago or that we will use the full majesty of the law to punish a man or woman because of their sexual proclivity.

That is not to suggest we all agree on every reform at every stage. There is a very good reason, for instance, why 'political correctness gone mad' has become one of the most overused phrases in the tabloid press. But the absurdity of a law weighing down on someone for making a harmless, if not very funny, joke about the Welsh or the Irish is a small price to pay for the relatively enlightened way in which we now think of real discrimination.

The dehumanising of one race by another has led to some of the greatest crimes against humanity the world has seen. At its extreme, it led to the gas chambers. With relatively few exceptions – the profoundly stupid or the irredeemably bigoted – we know in our hearts, in the depths of our conscience, that discrimination is wrong. It is as hard to imagine ourselves returning to the days when a landlady could put a 'no coloureds' sign in her boarding-house window as it is to contemplate sending a child up a chimney.

The other argument against the existence of a universal moral law or 'law of nature' is that different civilisations in different ages have had different moralities and still do. It sounds plausible, but there's not much evidence for it. As C. S. Lewis says, if you compare the moral teachings of, say, the ancient Egyptians, Babylonians, Hindus, Chinese, Greeks and Romans, what is really striking is how similar they were to each other and to our own rather than how different. Lewis offers this example of what a totally different morality might mean:

> Think of a country where people were admired for running away in battle or where a man felt proud of double-crossing all the people who had been kindest to him. You might just as well try to imagine a country where two and two make five. Men have differed as regards what people you ought to be unselfish to – whether it was only your own family or your fellow countryman or everyone – but they have always agreed that you ought not to put yourself first.

The language is a little dated now (Lewis was writing in the 1940s before women's liberation had been invented and no one objected to the use of 'men' rather than 'people') but his point is valid. The qualities we admire today in other human beings – courage, fidelity, truthfulness, generosity – are precisely the qualities that were lauded in *The Iliad* and *The Odyssey* or at the court of King Arthur or in the Outlaws' den of the *Just William* novels. They have remained unchanging through the millennia.

Remember, this is not about laws as enshrined on various statute books, which change all the time, this is about the moral law underpinning what it is to be a decent human being. Even the Roman Catholic Church – pretty resistant to change over the centuries – has altered its view of what it is to lead a moral life. It is not so long ago that the Church taught that to live morally meant obeying a set of laws. Now, says Professor Richard Gula of the Franciscan School of Theology, it has come to realise that the legal model for understanding the moral life and sin is deficient. It is no longer the case that sin is 'like a crime, a transgression of the law . . . akin to breaking the speed limit on the highway'. The Second Vatican Council said this:

In the depths of his conscience, man detects a law which he does not impose upon himself, but which holds him to obedience. Always summoning him to love good and avoid evil, the voice of conscience can, when necessary, speak to his heart more specifically: do this; shun that. For man has in his heart a law written by God. To obey it is the very dignity of man; according to it he will be judged. Conscience is the most secret core and sanctuary of a man. There he is: alone with God, whose voice echoes in his depths.

I have a few problems with some of that — hardly surprising given that I am not a Catholic and very much doubt that we will be 'judged' in the sense that the Church teaches — but it's hard to improve on most of the language. The idea of the voice of conscience as the 'most secret core and sanctuary' of a human being captures its essence.

In the medieval Church, conscience was spoken of as a function of the intellect or of the will. We used our brain to work out what was good and what was bad, and our will to choose which path to follow. Now the Church speaks of the heart rather than the head. Gula writes about the Biblical vision of the heart as 'that dimension of us which is most sensitive and open to others'. He says Paul, the chief New Testament author on the subject of conscience, describes it as 'our fundamental awareness of the difference between good and evil' and as a guide to loving decisions.

It's a bit odd, perhaps, that in this book about doubt I should quote approvingly from Catholic theology and the Gospels. You don't catch genuine twenty-four-carat atheists doing that – unless it's to pour scorn on the deluded souls who believe this guff. All of which makes me, I suppose, a pretty hopeless atheist – just as I was a pretty hopeless believer. The fact is, atheists have the best arguments. What they don't have – as far as I'm concerned – is much of a grasp on whatever it is that makes human beings what we are.

Self-evidently, biologists like Richard Dawkins know a thousand times more than most of us ever will about how our bodies work and how we evolved. It has been a long journey from the primordial swamp to Bach and Beethoven. At various points along the way we have acquired legs and high-functioning brains (not always evident, I grant you, in the case of some reality-television contestants) and the ability to create and destroy possessed by no other living creature. But there is that other mysterious attribute, about which so many scientists are curiously incurious.

There is our soul, our spirit, our conscience or whatever else you want to call it.

We are more than the sum of our genes – selfish or otherwise – but you might not think so if you read only the works and listened only to the words of the atheist evolutionists. They have precious little to say about our 'fundamental awareness of the difference between good and evil'. Nor do they have much to say about love. On the shelves in my office are rows of books about belief written by some of the great biologists, physicists, philosophers, sceptics and theologians of our time. Millions of words. A great store of knowledge and, sometimes, wisdom. But there is nothing that gets to the heart of it with the power and the beauty of these few verses from a book many of those writers affect to despise:

> If I speak in the tongues of men and of angels, but have not love, I am only a resounding gong or a clanging symbol. If I have the gift of prophecy and can fathom all mysteries and all knowledge, and if I have faith that can move mountains, but have not love, I am nothing. If I give all I possess to the poor and surrender my body to the flames, but have not love, I gain nothing.
>
> Love is patient, love is kind. It does not envy, it does not boast, it is not proud, it is not rude, it is

not self-seeking, it is not easily angered, it keeps no record of wrongs. Love does not delight in evil but rejoices with the truth. It always protects, always trusts, always hopes, always perseveres.

Love never fails. But where there are prophecies they will cease; where there are tongues they will be stilled; where there is knowledge, it will pass away. For we know in part and we prophesy in part, but when perfection comes the imperfect disappears. When I was a child, I talked like a child, I thought like a child, I reasoned like a child. When I was a man I put childish ways behind me.

Now we see but a poor reflection as in a mirror; then we shall see face to face. Now I know in part; then I shall know fully, even as I am fully known.

And now these three remain: faith, hope and love. But the greatest of these is love.

That's it, isn't it? Has there ever been a greater description of love? For St Paul of all people to pronounce that love is a greater virtue even than faith says a great deal. He could scarcely be more clear on the subject. When everything else is stripped away, it is love that remains. It is what makes us what we are. It distinguishes us from every other living creature. It was displayed by Liviu Librescu, Lisa Potts, Irena Sendlerova and every other human being who has acted out of pure selflessness at risk to themselves to save others. Christians would say the supreme example was Jesus. We cannot describe their actions in Darwinian terms.

The American biologist E. O. Wilson has been described as a genius of modern science and the natural heir to Darwin. He was a Southern Baptist but became an atheist by the time he went to university more than sixty years ago. Wilson talks about the existence of 'the transcendental experience at the heart of human nature'. I'd settle for that.

Something . . . Or Nothing?

19

For all their differences there are a couple of propositions on which atheist and believer can agree. One is that their dispute goes to the core of what it is to be human. As Hitchens puts it, the argument with faith is the foundation and origin of all arguments about philosophy, science, history and human nature. Another is that it will never be resolved – unless we reach a stage in our evolution when we can be confident that the human race has arrived at its destination and will develop no further. But we shall never reach that destination because to be alive is to evolve. So the argument will last for ever. But if the question of whether God exists can never be resolved, we can at least ask what sort of world this would be without religion.

It is possible that it would be a less violent place. Atheists say it's certain and they are right to point to the terrible things that have been done over the ages in the name of religion and the terrible things that are still being done. Yet the greatest horrors inflicted on humanity in the last century were inspired not by religion but by Communism. Here is how the historian Robert Service describes what the leaders of the Russian revolution did in October 1917:

> They instituted a red terror. They seized hold of an entire economy, persecuted all religious faith, imposed a one-ideology media and treated society as a force to be mobilised on their whim.

So religious faiths were the persecuted and not the persecutors. Stalin did not condemn millions to die in the gulags because of his religion. Mao did not cause even more millions to suffer and starve because of religion. Pol Pot did not murder millions in the killing fields of Cambodia because of religion. They did it in pursuit of their own ideology and to consolidate their hold on power. Hitler did not murder six million Jews because the Romans had nailed Jesus to a cross at their behest two thousand years ago. Their victims can be counted not in millions but tens of millions.

The bloodiest century in the history of mankind – from the carnage of the First World War to the genocide of Darfur – can be blamed on many things but religion comes some way down the list. Which is not to say that it has had no malign influence. It was an important factor in the horrors of Bosnia, Beirut and Northern Ireland – but only a factor. When one group of people sets out to murder or even eliminate another it is seldom because they worship different gods or follow a different path in the same religion. It is more often because there is real or perceived injustice some-where along the line and because their leaders exploit the religious differences to pursue their political ends.

I have spent a lot of time in Northern Ireland and regularly watched the streets of Belfast turn into battlefields with Protestants on one side of the line and Catholics on the other. I remember in the early 1970s being attacked by a mob, racing to the car to get away and having to grab the steering-wheel when a concrete slab smashed through the wind-screen and into the face of my cameraman, who was trying desperately to drive with blood pouring into his eyes. He was lucky it didn't kill him. The next day we sat in the neat parlour of a rioter's family and listened to their grievances. They were not con-cerned with religion – even though they called each other 'Prods' or 'Fenian bastards' – but about jobs and housing and a partisan police force. And now that those things are being dealt with, the rioting and killing has stopped. Ian Paisley may never share a church pew with the hated Papists, but he is sharing government.

Western politicians warn us that Northern Ireland or even Bosnia were little local difficulties compared to the threat posed today by militant Islamists or, if you prefer Hitchens' description of them, 'the mirthless cretins of jihad'. Hassan Butt was a member of the British Jihadi Network (BJN), which he describes as a series of semi-autonomous British Muslim terrorist groups linked by a single ideology. They are, he says, 'fighting for the creation of a revolutionary state that would eventually bring Islamic justice to the world'. By a process of complicated and bizarre reasoning, they calculate that the whole world is *Dar ul-Kufr*, which means the Land of Unbelief, and they have declared war on it. That, in turn, means the world becomes a Land of War, *Dar ul-Harb*. Here's how Butt explains it:

> It allows any Muslim to destroy the sanctity of the five rights that every human is granted under Islam: life, wealth, land, mind and belief. In *Dar ul-Harb*, anything goes, including the treachery and cowardice of attacking civilians.

That they represent a threat is beyond doubt. What is also clear is that they do not represent mainstream Islam. Ed Husain, in his book *The Islamist*, tries to 'reclaim' Islam and, as he puts it, 'separate the ancient spiritual path from a post-colonial political ideology'. It will not be easy. The 'post-colonial' Middle East became a fertile breeding ground for terrorism. When extremists manage to win the support of ordinary people it is less to do with religion and much more to do with political failure.

In 1979 Ayatollah Khomeini would not have been welcomed back to Iran as the nation's saviour if the monarchs who had ruled for so long had given the Iranians the freedom, stability and prosperity they expected, and if the Western powers had interfered less. The Taliban were greeted as heroes when they took over in Afghanistan because the country had endured so many years of misrule and invasions by foreign powers. It's worth remembering that the West armed Muslim fundamentalists in their fight against the Soviet invaders — only to see those arms turned against themselves.

As I write, the militant organisation Hamas has been seizing power in Gaza. Hamas is part of the Muslim Brotherhood, an international movement dedicated to creating a single global Islamic state. But that was not why the Palestinians in Gaza voted for them. It was because the leaders of the ruling Fatah Party were corrupt and incompetent. If they had succeeded the fundamentalists would have failed.

No extremist religious organisation has ever taken control of a stable, democratic society – unless, that is, you buy the Hitchens line that Fascism is a manifestation of religion. It is only when people are suffering and feel threatened by outsiders or oppressed by the system that they give their support to extremists bent on violence. If the Taliban are regaining support today in parts of Afghanistan it is partly because the promises made to the people after they were overthrown in 2001 by an international coalition have not been met. That does not justify their foul deeds – they some- times murder schoolgirls for the crime of wanting to be educated – but it helps to explain why they get even a modicum of support in some areas.

Even in Iraq, it is worth remembering that the Shiites and Sunnis who murder each other in such vast numbers today have often lived in relative harmony, working together, even marrying each other. But Saddam's vile dictatorship was over- thrown, bloody anarchy took its place and the extremists were able to exploit the mayhem with the hideous results we see today.

You can hardly argue with atheists who say that if religion did not exist organisations like Al-Qaeda and the Muslim Brotherhood would not exist. But something else would. History is pretty clear about this: if enough people feel a sufficiently powerful sense of grievance, then sooner or later the lid will blow – however tightly their oppressors try to screw it down. Sometimes the effect will be beneficial and sometimes it will be disastrous. Sometimes religion will fill the vacuum, sometimes ideologies such as Fascism or Communism. Hitchens deals with this inconvenient fact by claiming that there's not really much to choose between totalitarianism and theism. He quotes George Orwell: 'A totalitarian state is in effect a theocracy.' There may be something in that – if I were a woman I'm not sure whether I'd have chosen to live in the old Soviet Union or Saudi Arabia – but that is *not* the choice.

The historian John Gray makes the point that it's easy to forget how during the twentieth century terror was used on a vast scale by secular regimes. Today, he says, suicide attacks are automatically linked with a belief in martyrdom followed by paradise in the afterlife, yet they were developed by people with no such beliefs:

> Islamist terrorists are continuing a modern Western tradition of using systematic violence to transform society. The roots of contemporary terrorism are in radical Western ideology – especially Leninism – far more than religion.

According to Professor Gray, Lenin saw himself as belonging to a European revolutionary tradition that began with the French Jacobins. In 1793 the Jacobins unleashed what became known as the 'reign of terror', executing perhaps forty thousand people over the following ten months. Gray says Lenin's only quarrel with what they did was that they had not been 'sufficiently merciless'.

He and Trotsky set up concentration camps and instituted a system of hostages to ensure obedience in suspect groups. Between 1917 and 1923 he had about two hundred thousand people killed. But hasn't that sort of secular terrorism died out? Not at all, says Gray. Suicide bombings may now be the Islamist technique of choice, but it was the Tamil Tigers – a Marxist-Leninist group in Sri Lanka – that devised it. It was the Tamil Tigers that developed the explosive belt worn by Islamic *jihad* suicide bombers, and up to the Iraq war, the Tigers had committed more such attacks than any other organisation.

In his book *Black Mass: Apocalyptic Religion and the Death of Utopia*, Gray argues that Islamic terrorists have taken from Lenin a modern 'faith' that is not found in either traditional Islam or Christianity: the idea that through the systematic deployment of violence, a new world can be brought into being. Terrible things happened in the guise of religion in medieval Europe, but it was never imagined that the use of violence could initiate a perfect society or rid the world of immemorial evils.

> Faith is dangerous . . . but fanaticism comes in many guises. We would do well to remember that it was secular faith that inspired much of the terror of the last century. The fantasy that society can be progressively transformed by violence inspired some of humanity's worst crimes, and it casts a poisonous spell today.

Clearly the world would be a better place without religious extremism of any kind, but for atheists to claim that without religion peace and harmony would reign is patently absurd. It's not the Bible that proves that. It's the history books.

20

When I started thinking about this book I fell into the habit of asking almost everyone I met if they believed in God. I was mildly embarrassed about it in the early days. I was afraid they'd suspect me of trying to convert them – one way or the other. Most of the time I expected them to tell me to clear off and mind my own business. And why not? Aren't we supposed to be reticent in this country when it comes to talking about such matters? My mother would no more have talked about her beliefs than she would have broken wind in the corner shop. Even today it is regarded in some quarters as a taboo subject.

Alastair Campbell gave one of his few unequivocally straight answers while he was Tony Blair's master of spin when he was asked about the prime minister's religion. 'We don't do God,' he said. That was a bit odd because we all knew that Tony Blair was a devout Christian with a leaning towards the Roman Catholic Church. Indeed, by the time you read this it's possible he will have converted to Catholicism. But on balance it's probably a good thing that British politicians don't 'do God'.

In the United States they do – in a big way – and we don't want to go down that road. The religious right there has the power to destroy any politician who doesn't give acceptable answers on abortion, homosexuality or any of the other things that cause Southern Baptists to foam at the mouth. And there's something deeply worrying about the president of the most powerful nation in the world allegedly believing he has a direct line to the Almighty and will do as he tells him – especially when it comes to invading foreign countries.

But to judge by my own experience, the old reticence on the part of most people in this country is disappearing. Maybe it's a question of you-show-me-yours-and-I'll-show-you-mine. If someone is prepared to say what he believes or does not believe, as I did for my Radio 4 series, others seem happy to join in. I don't think anyone flatly refused to tell me. But here's the interesting thing: it was only the atheists who seemed absolutely certain. Of course, this proves nothing: it's purely anecdotal and statistically worthless. But it does point in an interesting direction.

The main target of the militant atheists seems to be the educated middle class – for the obvious reason that it's they who are likely to read the books and watch the programmes. If enough clever people state something with absolute certainty – and with lots of 'evidence' to back it up – it is likely to have an effect. Just as most teenagers are terrified of being seen to be different from their peers, many of their elders and betters are nervous at being exposed for not having read the right books or taken on board the latest, fashionable views. Or it might be that they sense the climate is changing and whereas they had been a bit reluctant to admit their uncertainties a couple of generations ago they think it's safe now to come out of the closet.

Whatever the reason, even people I have always known to be devout, churchgoing Christians seemed keen to distance themselves a little from their religion. 'Yes, well, I'm pretty sure there's some greater power out there, but I don't know whether I really believe in what you'd call "God",' seems to sum up most people's response. You can almost see the quotation marks hanging in the air as they speak.

My old friend Rod Liddle has always shuffled his feet a bit when we get on to the subject – as we often do – after the first couple of drinks. In fact, Rod may be the perfect illustration of my point. He is one of the cleverest and best-read men I know – iconoclastic, fiercely independent. I doubt he has ever formed an opinion because it happens to be fashionable. Anyone who has read one of his many newspaper and magazine columns will know that he's not exactly a member of the 'on the one hand . . . but on the other' school of journalism – which is one of the things that makes him such a good columnist. Yet in 2006 he made a documentary for Channel 4 called *The Problem With Atheism* and here's how he ended it:

> The true scientific position, of course, is that there may be a God, or there may not be a God. Why can't we leave it at that?

Well, we can. Of course we can. In fact, as a card-carrying doubter, I think that is the *only* way we can leave it. But Rod believes in God. And what worries me is that a climate is growing in which people who believe are becoming reluctant to say so. In fact, Rod agrees with that analysis:

> Atheists have become terribly preoccupied with destroying God and religion and it's the absolute certitude with which they do this – and the

contempt sprayed upon those who fail to share
their disbelief – that worries me a little bit.
History has shown us that it is not religion so
much that's a problem but any system of thought
which insists that one group of people are in-
violably in the right, whereas the others are in
the wrong and thus must somehow be punished.

I couldn't have put it better myself – which is
why I almost wish Rod had ended his excellent
documentary with a more characteristic 'I know
what I believe so you atheists can just sod off!' But
maybe he was right to exercise a little restraint.
Argument is a good thing. Always. About everything. You can't have too much of it. It's when we
stop arguing that we start fighting. It's the intem-
perate nature of the atheist argument that is unacceptable.

Steve Jones is Professor of Genetics at University
College London. He has always struck me as a
civilised human being: thoughtful and humane.
But he surprised me with a contribution he made
to the great religious debate in a letter to the
Guardian in which he gave a definition of evil.
Evil, he said, was teaching children things you
know to be wrong. That really is quite extraor-

dinary. Doesn't it depend on what, exactly, you are teaching them? It is certainly wicked to teach children that Hitler was right to murder Jews or that people who do not share your own faith should be put to death. But to teach children that there was a good man called Jesus who was killed by some bad men but came alive again and then went to heaven because he was really the son of God and loved us all? Are we really, honestly, saying that teaching this is evil?

That – very roughly – is what my little boy believes. He obviously doesn't get it from me and I assume that he picks it up at school. The head-master assures me that they do not indoctrinate the children, but the critical faculties of a six-year-old are not exactly finely honed so I suppose he may have accepted the Gospel stories in the same way he accepts the teacher's description of proven histor-ical events. Maybe she should have shown a little more scepticism or at least entered a few caveats. Maybe she has allowed her own beliefs to influence her teaching. It's been known. Or maybe he picked it up from one of his churchgoing peers. Either way, it's not as if he had been indoctrinated into some evil cult and will one day murder us all in our beds.

When we talk about it, I tell him that some people believe the Bible stories and some don't. I have no doubt that, as he grows older, he will decide for himself and if he continues to believe, that's fine. If he doesn't, that's fine too. But the idea that it was 'evil' to teach it to him in the first place is crazy. A letter in response to Jones from Ian Flintoff put it rather well:

> Lying to children is evil, says Steve Jones. So no more 'You'll get well soon, darling', or 'You'll love your spinach' or 'Once upon a time there was a little girl called Little Red Riding Hood'. What a cold, dull, flat and colourless world of the imagination poor Steve and his buddies must inhabit. Give me the gods, the spirits, the myths and Father Christmas any time. They make science so much more interesting and valuable.

Let me try to sum up the attitude of those militant atheists who seem to hold believers in contempt:

1. Believers are mostly naïve or stupid. Or, at least, they're not as clever as atheists.
2. The few clever ones are pathetic because they need a crutch to get them through life.
3. They are also pathetic because they can't accept the finality of death.

4. They have been brainwashed into believing. There is no such thing as a 'Christian child', for instance – just a child whose parents have had her baptised.

5. They have been bullied into believing.

6. If we don't wipe out religious belief by next Thursday week, civilisation as we know it is doomed.

7. Trust me: I'm an atheist.

I make no apology if I have over-simplified their views with that little list: it's what they do to believers all the time. So let's answer each of those points:

1. This is so clearly untrue it's barely worth bothering with. Dawkins was actually reduced to producing a 'study' by Mensa, which purported to show an inverse relationship between intelligence and belief. He also claimed that only a very few members of the Royal Society believe in a personal god. So what? Some believers are undoubtedly stupid (witness the creationists) but I've met one or two atheists I wouldn't trust to change a lightbulb or post a letter. All this stuff proves is that cleverness is not the same as wisdom.

2. Don't we all? Some use booze rather than the Bible. It doesn't prove anything about either.

3. Maybe, but it doesn't mean they're wrong. Count the number of atheists in the foxholes or the cancer wards.

4. True, and many children reject it when they get older. But many others stay with it.

5. This is also true in many cases but you can't actually bully someone into believing – just into pretending to believe.

6. Of course the mad mullahs are dangerous and extreme Islamism is a threat to be taken seriously. But we've survived monotheist religion for four thousand years or so, and I can think of one or two other things that are a greater threat to civilisation.

7. Why?

For those of us who are neither believers nor atheists it can be very difficult. Doubters are left in the deeply unsatisfactory position of finding the existence of God unprovable and deeply implausible, and the comfort of faith unachievable. But at the same time we find the reality of belief undeniable. It's bad enough being a failed Christian – sneered at by atheists and believers.

It's even worse being what I suppose you could

call someone like me – a failed atheist. Or maybe it's not. That's what Giles Fraser has been calling himself for years and he happens to be an Anglican vicar. He's also a regular on *Thought for the Day*, writes for the *Guardian*, has had the central character in a West End play (*On Religion*) based on him and teaches philosophy at Oxford. So he ticks lots of boxes. He's clever too. Indeed, you might have expected him to end up in the Dawkins camp. Why didn't he?

Here's his own description of himself when he was younger: 'a bolshy kid who discovered Marx at school and gave myself over to it hook, line and sinker'. He sold *Socialist Worker* on street corners, took 'the text' almost literally and condemned 'heretics' who had a different take on Communism. During the miners' strike in the mid-1980s he realised what a sham it all was – 'a privileged public schoolboy like me playing at politics', as he told me. His 'faith' in Marxism collapsed but he remained an atheist.

It was his interest in atheism that made him take religion seriously. He did his PhD on Nietzsche, and theology became 'a sort of hobby'. He immersed himself in the great theologians and that was when his conversion happened – except that he doesn't like that word. He regards the language of conversion as 'a bit creepy'. What happened was that after years of looking into theology from the outside he discovered that he was on the inside looking out. He realised that he believed in God. He seems genuinely puzzled by it.

I have described Giles Fraser in some detail because he is the sort of religious believer whom atheists find difficult to deal with: one of those moving targets they can't quite fix in their crosshairs. There are many like him in the Anglican Church who share his scorn (if not contempt) for the more traditional approach to Christianity. He is embarrassed by 'stupid Christians thinking they know more about the nature of the universe than clever atheists like Dawkins'. Ask him to prove that God exists – one of the things he teaches at Oxford – and he cheerfully admits that he can't. He goes further:

The so-called proofs of God's existence are all rubbish.

Ask him if the resurrection of Jesus Christ really happened and he says:

Umm . . . dunno . . . can't prove it.

Ask him about evangelical Christians and he snorts quite loudly:

Evangelicals have misunderstood the Bible. They turn it into some bloody Ikea manual.

Ask him to sum up the state of battle between militant believers and militant atheists and he says:

Atheists have the best arguments, which makes belief such a precarious thing.

And so it goes. In hours of conversation over the kitchen table I have tried hard to pick a proper argument with him about theology – as I say, he teaches it – but I have failed. That's partly because he freely acknowledges that theology is not some sort of intellectual platform on which faith can be built. He quotes Augustine – theology is 'faith seeking understanding' – which means you get your faith first and then try to make sense of it, rather than the other way round. And faith is not a belief that certain propositions about the world are true. It is not grounded in rational argument and neither is there any good line of reasoning that can persuade one to believe. Belief just isn't like that, says Fraser. So what is it like? Why does a believer believe?

I'm not talking here about the 'belief' that propels a middle-class family to start going to church because that's the only way to get little Tarquin into the rather good Church of England primary instead of that ghastly school at the end of the road. Nor am I thinking of the upwardly mobile young City dealer who signs on for the Alpha Course because he'd rather like, y'know, a bit of spiritual hand-holding. Or those sad people whose lives are so horribly empty they might as easily have become pagans or morris dancers. And I'm absolutely not talking about those who 'believe' because they are afraid of what will happen to them if they don't. I'm talking about ordinary people leading ordinary lives, with the sort of hopes and fears we all share, who have found a faith in whatever it happens to be and have held on to it. Their faith is part of them and they cannot imagine their lives without it. Why?

What's interesting is that you get much the same answer to that question whether it comes from a philosopher/vicar like Giles Fraser or a theologian/ archbishop like Rowan Williams or an old lady who left school at fourteen, has never read a book on philosophy or theology in her life and wouldn't know the difference between an ontological argument and a pork pie. Why should she? Theology, as Fraser says, is not the foundation of faith. The Archbishop and the little old lady down the road might use a different vocabulary to try to explain why they believe, but it comes to the same thing in the end. They believe because they believe. This is not about intellect or learning: it's more basic than that. It is both more profound and more simple.

I suspect that on the most primitive level it is not all that different from the little scrap of blanket that so many small children rely on. They need it whenever they get tired or life looks a bit threatening. I say 'need', not 'want', quite deliberately: every parent who has had a child with a comfort blanket knows what I mean.

I invite you to imagine the impossibly grand figure of the Archbishop of Canterbury – mitred and robed, holder of an ancient and powerful office, head of the worldwide Anglican Church, crowner of monarchs – sitting on the steps of Canterbury Cathedral with his thumb stuck in his mouth, stroking his bearded cheek with the little bit of satin at the edge of his comfort blanket. It's not easy, I grant you, and this image may not do a great deal for the dignity of the primate's office, but the comfort blanket is not a million miles away from what religion offers at its most simplistic. Strip from Christianity the notion of proof, evidence and historical events (or non-events) and what drives belief has little to do with the head and a great deal to do with the heart.

*　　*　　*

Many atheists, as my list suggests, say that people believe because of the way they were brought up: children are credulous and accept what they are told. As they grow older they get rid of their comfort blankets and often the beliefs with which they were inculcated. But not everyone does that – and even those who do may return to belief, in one form or another, in later life. There remains what the atheist philosopher A. C. Grayling calls 'the lingering splinter in the mind . . . a sense of yearning for the absolute'.

I'm sure he's right about that. There is a profound longing for something that will stimulate and satisfy them emotionally and spiritually. Grayling and other atheists understand that longing perfectly well, but what puzzles them is why it cannot be satisfied by pottering about in the garden, a walk in the hills, watching a sunset, listening to a piece of great music. Yet that misses the point. Believers may very well find comfort and solace in all those things – I remember how Rowan Williams almost pounced on me as if I had made a great admission when I mentioned that listening to Bach can be a spiritual experience – but where atheists are wrong is in failing to recognise and understand that most believers want something else as well. It is hard to talk to Christians about religion without them eventually using the word 'love'.

Grayling co-wrote the play *On Religion* in which one of the lead characters, Tom – who is loosely based on Giles Fraser – decides to be ordained in the Anglican Church. In the play his mother is a fiercely intelligent but unpleasant, rebarbative atheist with a contempt for religion. She gets the best arguments, but Tom is the character you warm to. One of his main scenes is taken from Giles Fraser's own life. Fraser told me about it:

> The night before I got married my brother sat me down in an Indian restaurant and (too many beers) got me to make a list on a napkin of why this girl was the right person for me to marry. One side of the napkin had all the pros and the other side the cons. What was fascinating about the list was that nothing I could write down – kind, pretty, warm, sexy, etc. – could ever add up to 'I love her.' To marry and make the love commitment is the nearest thing to faith I know because it is something done with the same degree of risk. Would a person who needed everything fully evidenced and rationally demonstrated ever be in a position to say, 'I love you'?

Couldn't a Dawkins-type figure make a case for love being a fiction, a function of human need, a function of biology and selfish genes? He may have many useful and persuasive things to say but there is something deeply mistaken about thinking love is simply reducible to the chemistry of the brain. Love, like faith, is to make more of a commitment than one can prove. But there is a truth to it that I won't – indeed can't – back away from. Of course, there is much to say about all of this and I can think of a dozen reasons why faith and love might look different. But the truth of both is, for me, found in the poetry, not in the science.

I started this book by suggesting that we may be at another religious turning-point, with the apathy of the past half-century replaced by a more aggressive approach from both militant believers and militant atheists. In the United States the atheists are a beleaguered minority, overwhelmed by the powerful Christian Right. Here, it is Christianity that has been mostly on the defensive. Shortly after Charles Darwin stood the world on its head in 1859 with his stunning theory of evolution, Matthew Arnold wrote a poem called 'Dover Beach'. Here are the last two verses:

The Sea of Faith
Was once, too, at the full, and round earth's
    shore
Lay like the folds of a bright girdle furled.
But now I only hear
Its melancholy, long, withdrawing roar,
Retreating, to the breath
Of the night-wind, down the vast edges drear
And naked shingles of the world.

Ah, love, let us be true
To one another! for the world, which seems
To lie before us like a land of dreams,
So various, so beautiful, so new,
Hath really neither joy, nor love, nor light,
Nor certitude, nor peace, nor help for pain;
And we are here as on a darkling plain
Swept with confused alarms of struggle and
    flight,
Where ignorant armies clash by night.

Arnold was right to suggest that Darwin changed everything and to assume that his theories
would stand the test of time. Some have been
challenged over the past few years – it has been
shown that sudden changes can come about in
some species in a single generation – but what he
proved conclusively for everyone capable of ra-

tional thought was that God did not create the world in six days a few thousand years ago and dinosaurs did not roam the Garden of Eden with Adam and Eve. More seriously, it enabled atheists to claim (as Richard Dawkins would many years later) that God could not have existed at all. It proved that life evolved over vast periods of time, simple organisms undergoing gradual changes and becoming more and more complex. That, says Dawkins, proves that there cannot have been a divine being before we crawled out of the swamp because it would have to have been more complex than the organisms that followed it.

No wonder Arnold imagined the 'melancholy, long, withdrawing' roar of religion. But surely he was wrong to see the world of the future with 'neither joy, nor love, nor light, nor certitude, nor peace, nor help for pain'. The certitude has gone, that's for sure, but faith has not withdrawn. It may have staged a few tactical retreats and even lost many battles, but it's still there. And it is still helping vast numbers of people in pain. I came across one recently.

It was a blog reproduced on the *Daily Telegraph*'s website by a man called Phil Stoddart. His two beloved daughters, Claire and Jenny, were killed by a driver who was on the wrong side of the road and travelling fast after a night in his club. Claire was eighteen and Jenny was fifteen. They had just finished their exams, each with the best marks in their class. Mr Stoddart and his wife Heather were told about the crash and rushed to the hospital, passing the wreckage of their daughters' car on their way. Here is what he wrote on the website:

> They had Jenny breathing but only artificially. They'd let us know more shortly and left us with a cup of tea. We knew in our hearts that Claire was dead and I sensed that Jenny was gone too. I found it hard to sit down . . . so I wandered out for a few moments in the fresh daylight air. Lord I so need you. I went back in quickly and sat with Heather who could barely move and we prayed. This was it, this was the moment God met with us in that little room. We prayed and spoke to him and for my part I knew then for sure that they were both gone to be with him and I think Heather knew as well. How did we feel? Well, calm and peace came to us. We were assured they were with him and a strong conviction of this was upon us. A strength came into me and focus and purpose. The nurse returned with the verdict [from a brain scan] from Addenbrookes: they

said she was brain dead and took us to see her. When we got to the bed there was a curtain around it. We asked to be alone because I wanted to pray over her with no interference. Finally we stood either side of the bed and looked on her face. There was a swollen look to her but peaceful as though sleeping. I prayed because I knew God could bring her back if he wanted. We prayed, I heard his calm, reassuring voice again: 'No, she's home with me.' We said goodbye and looked at the bed again. She was no longer there. The body is a tent and she had left it. We knew that. We left the bedside and asked the nurse not to keep the life support on for our sake.

Of course, atheists and agnostics will not believe it was the voice of God that Mr Stoddart heard. How can we when we do not believe in a God that speaks individually to us? But so what? What does it matter whether we believe it or not? Or whether Richard Dawkins and every other militant atheist who ever fired a broadside at religion thinks his faith is a delusion? If it has given strength to a mother and father to bear an unimaginable loss, it can only be a good thing. Their faith also gave them the strength to forgive the man who had killed their daughters – something that would be beyond most of us, I suspect. But how much better than being eaten away by anger and bitterness for the rest of their lives.

Let me be charitable to the militant atheists. I do not believe they would wish to deny Mr and Mrs Stoddart and millions of others the comfort their faith has brought them. Yet they regard them as delusional. So where would they suggest they turn for comfort? To the professionals, perhaps? The grief counsellors, the psychotherapists, the peddlers of pills that banish depression and grief with one quick swallow? Are Mr and Mrs Stoddart any more deluded for turning to their God to help them through the agony of their grief than all those who worshipped at the shrine of Freud and tried to find meaning to their lives on the analyst's couch? I doubt it.

Militant atheists seem to have enormous difficulty in understanding why so many people – many of them just as clever as they are – manage to live by their beliefs. Here's what Richard Dawkins told Laurie Taylor in *New Humanist* magazine:

> I don't know what it would mean to say that we live by faith in our daily life. There is, I suppose,

a sense that we are sometimes too busy to reason everything out, but otherwise I don't know what it means.

It seems to me that he misses the point entirely. It's not necessarily that people are too busy to reason things out. It's more that they don't want to. They *want* to believe. In spite of the terrible things that have been done in the name of God over the millennia, religious belief brings immeasurable comfort. In 2007 Dawkins landed himself in trouble when he attacked Peter Kay for what he had written in his autobiography *The Sound of Laughter*. Kay, who was brought up as a Roman Catholic, does not believe in the divinity of Christ but does 'believe in a God of some kind, in some sort of higher being'. He says he finds it 'very comforting'.

Dawkins would have none of that. 'How can you take seriously someone who likes to believe something because he finds it "comforting"?' he demanded. After that was reported in the newspapers Dawkins suggested that he had not set out to ridicule Kay and had been stitched up by a clever public-relations operator. That's entirely possible: one should never underestimate the ruthlessness of a PR operator with a product to sell. But anyone who has read *The God Delusion* will know that it's not a million miles from what he thinks.

Like Kay, I do not accept the divinity of Jesus. I do not believe that his mother was made pregnant by the Holy Ghost, that he was resurrected after his death on the cross, or that he physically ascended to heaven. But that belief enriches the lives of many.

It does not make them stupid, let alone deluded. It makes them human. Their faith gives them a context into which they can fit their lives and a hope of better things to come – if not in this world, then the next. And if the next world turns out not to exist . . . well, they'll never know, will they?

I have talked to many people for the purpose of writing this book – eminent theologians, historians, scientists, clerics – but let me finish with a woman called Mrs Buchanan. You'll never have heard of her and I can't give you her first name because I knew her in the days when children did not call adults by their first names. Even my mother called her Mrs Buchanan or Mrs B. Her life – I now realise – was sad. The one thing she and her husband wanted above everything else was children, and that was not to be. There was no IVF in the 1950s.

My own mother had five children. There was often very little money and sometimes she struggled to cope. Mrs Buchanan was always there to help. She was a stalwart of the Mothers' Union at our local church and she regarded it as her duty. Monday was washing day, and every Monday afternoon she would turn up – her hat pinned firmly to her hair – to help with the ironing. The hat stayed on. Outside her own home I never saw her without it.

Mr and Mrs Buchanan were an unremarkable couple – quiet, honest, decent, God-fearing. They worked hard – I have Mr Buchanan's old teak toolbox beside the desk in my office to this day – and made no demands of anyone. The Church was an important part of their lives, not that you would ever hear them talking about their belief. It was simply there and they were glad of it. It provided structure and, I think, some meaning to their lives.

What have the Buchanans and the millions like them to do with the militant atheists and their supercharged campaign against religion? The latter will say it is irrelevant. They will probably accuse me of viewing the world through the rose-tinted spectacles of half a century ago when society was altogether less cynical and world-weary. They will say that people like the Buchanans – if they still exist – would be better off if only they could see religion and the Church for the nonsense that it is. And they'd be wrong. For them, what matters is what can be proved to be true. That's it. But in the real world, outside the walls of their intellectual ivory towers, that's *not* it.

This is not an intellectual game. Even if we know what is true – and we don't – you cannot reduce life to a set of provable realities. Humanity is too complex for that. In the end, it comes down to whether the world would be a better place without religion – and that is a matter of judgement, not certainty. Yes, we loathe and fear the fanaticism that leads to a man strapping a bomb to his body and blowing up other human beings. But we should also fear a world in which the predominant values are materialism and consumerism, and the greatest aspiration of too many children is to become a 'celebrity'. It's naïve to assume that we will ever return to the days when you had to climb Everest or run the first four-minute mile to achieve fame. Television has seen to that. But Paris Hilton? The existence of religion can offer some balance in a society obsessed with image, which turns vacuity into virtue.

It's worth noting that militant atheists who savage religion for the poisonous effect it has on our lives invariably have nice things to say about the religious believers they know personally. The French philosopher Michel Onfray, who has added yet another book to the atheist canon with his *In Defence of Atheism*, writes about a journey he made to the Mauritanian desert with his driver, a devout Muslim he called Abdou. This is how Onfray describes Abdou:

> A man of near-saintly ways – considerate, tactful, willing to share, ever mindful of others, gentle and calm, at peace with himself, with others and with the world.

One night he watched Abdou pray beneath a full moon:

> Slowly, as though impelled by the ancestral movements of the planet, he knelt, lowered his forehead to the ground and prayed. Light from dead stars reached down to us in the hot desert night. I felt that I was witnessing a primitive ritual, similar to humankind's earliest act of worship.

Onfray argued at length with Abdou about the Koran. Did he really believe that its fantastic description of paradise was meant to be taken literally? Yes, he did. But before entering paradise, said Abdou, he would have accounts to settle. He had committed a terrible error.

Ah, said Onfray, what sort of 'error'? A crime? A murder? A mortal sin, as Christians say? No. What Abdou had once done was to drive too fast and had run over a jackal. He had committed the sacrilege of killing an animal when he had no need to eat it.

We may shake our heads a little at that. Poor chap, thinking he will be denied paradise because he drove too fast on a desert road. Clearly deluded. But even if he is . . . does it matter? I wonder how his God could possibly deny someone salvation because of a minor accident, but what I believe doesn't matter a row of beans to Abdou and nor should it. The fact is, the world is a slightly better place for people like him, with his respect for all living things, and the Buchanans and the Stoddarts.

As I write these last few sentences I look out from my office onto the tennis court facing my house. It is a hot, muggy summer's day and a group of young women are playing. They are clothed from head to toe in black, their jeans poking out from beneath the chadors. They look peculiarly ungainly and they must be stifling. As a non-Muslim it seems a bit odd and a bit alien to me, but so does a lot of other things – such as the fashionably dressed young people who get so drunk on Friday and Saturday nights you have to think twice about venturing into the town centre. We each make our own choices.

One choice is to accept the conclusion reached by Jean-Paul Sartre in *The Age of Reason*:

There is no purpose to existence, only nothingness.

That is a perfectly rational conclusion if, like me, you cannot accept that we exist in order to worship God. It is very hard to see any purpose in a world where an accident of birth determines whether a child leads a long and healthy life or dies an early death in grinding poverty; a world of hunger and war and disease; a world that we may be destroying through our own greed and stupidity. But however much he may appeal to our reason, Sartre's conclusion is too bleak for me.

Trite it may be, but most of us can see the beauty as well as the horrors of the world and, sometimes, humanity at its most noble. We sense a spiritual element in that nobility and in the miracle of unselfish love and sacrifice, something beyond our conscious understanding. You don't need to be an eastern mystic or a devout religious believer to feel that. We should not – we must not – be browbeaten by arrogant atheists and meekly accept their deluded label. They are no more capable of understanding this most profound mystery than a small child making his first awe-inspiring discoveries.

As for the fanatics – religious or secular – history suggests they succeed only to the extent that we allow ourselves to be defeated by our own irrational fear. Even Christopher Hitchens believes that extreme Islamism is a sign of weakness, not strength. For every fanatic there are countless ordinary, decent people who believe in their own version of a benevolent God and wish no harm to anyone. Many of them regard it as their duty to try to make the world a better place. It is too easy to blame the evils of the world on belief in God. In the end, if we make a mess of things, we shall have ourselves to blame – not religion and not God. After all, he doesn't exist. Does he?